CONTENTS

4 North Parade, Bath, BA1 1LF, UK

First Published: 2010

CONTENTS

Discover all the animals on the farm!
FARM
ANIMALS

WHAT IS A FARM?

A farm is a large area of land that is mainly used to grow crops, and to rear animals like cows, sheep and pigs.

Animal Farms

Not all farms grow crops. Some farms rear animals like cows, pigs, sheep, chickens and other fowl. These are specialised farms and require equipment to handle a large stock of animals, such as tractors. More animals are being bred than ever before, to meet the demands of the world, which means an increase in the production of milk, meat, eggs and other farm animal derived products.

Poultry Farms

Poultry farms raise chickens, turkeys, geese, ducks and other fowl. Poultry farms raise these fowl mainly for meat while layer poultry farms raise fowl to produce eggs. Poultry farming is a specialised business. Breeders need to choose the right species to get the desired fowl. So the breeder is able to raise chickens with less or more fat, or ducks that yield more eggs! Though poultry farms mainly produce meat and eggs, they also yield feathers for pillows and quilts.

Dairy Farms

Dairy farms breed cows, buffaloes, goats and sheep to produce large quantities of milk and meat. The animals are often fed special nutritious food to increase productivity and meat. In fact, some dairy farms even grow their own feed like corn and hay that the animals eat. Some dairy farms also crossbreed species to produce new species. Dairy farms usually sell off male calves, because they don't produce milk.

COWS

Cows are among the most important farm animals. They provide us with milk, meat and leather. Cows can also serve as draft animals and help some to plough fields and pull carts.

Farm Friend

Cows belong to the family of bovines which also includes water buffaloes, bisons, yaks and spiral horned antelopes. Cows are among the first animals to be domesticated for agricultural purposes. Cows are quite harmless but if you pester them too much you might get a kick or a butt from their head! Cows are mainly useful for the nutritious milk they give. Their flesh, called beef, is also relished as food by many. Their hide is used as leather to make products like shoes and bags. Since they are quite sturdy and can also be easily trained, in many parts of the world they are often a major helping hand on the farm, carrying loads and ploughing fields.

◀Cows are the most important dairy animals and are used for a variety of purposes

Food and Shelter

Cows on the farm must be taken care of properly. They should be provided with good shelter and nutritious food. They should be housed in wooden or brick barns or cowsheds. Good food is vital to good health. So cows must be fed juicy grass and hay as a part of their diet. They should also be fed an occasional diet of grain. Cows also like to graze on open pastures. In fact, cattle are often allowed to graze on large patches of grass. This ensures a good use of land that might not be suitable for growing other crops.

Shelters for cows should be safe, clean and hygienic

Milking a Cow

Cows provide us with milk. This milk can be used to make various dairy products like cheese, cream, butter and yoghurt. But, for this, cows need to be milked using a proper technique. They should be milked by hand or machines. Milking machines are often used on farms. These machines can extract large quantities of milk and are vital for producing dairy products on a large scale. These milking machines also process the milk in sealed containers. This makes the process more hygienic and also prevents the milk from getting spoilt.

Extracting milk with the help of machines increases the amount obtained from a cow

HORSES

Horses are among the most magnificent and beautiful looking animals. They have a lot of strength and stamina and are very fast runners, making them an asset to many farms.

Draught Horses

Most breeds of horses can carry humans on their backs with ease and can also be harnessed to pull objects. Horses are increasingly being selectively bred for specific jobs: there are lighter horses for racing and heavier ones that are used on farms. Farm horses are known as draught horses. These horses are large, healthy, muscular and powerful. They are also extremely adept at performing hard tasks like ploughing, carrying heavy loads and pulling carts.

Eat Well to Stay Well

Horses are kept in stables on farms, which are safe and comfortable for them. Dirty stables breed diseases and so must be cleaned regularly. As draught horses work very hard they need to be fed adequately. A typical diet comprises of a bulk of roughage like hay and grass and some concentrates like oats and barley, which provide them with energy for heavy physical labour.

▲*Draught horses are used to perform a large number of heavy tasks at the farm*

▲Horses need to be given a complete diet of hay, grass and oats to keep them healthy and fit

▲Shirehorses are used as draught animals as well as for public shows

CREATURE PROFILE

Common Name:	Suffolk punch
Colour:	Shades ranging from light gold to dark brown
Height:	1.6–1.7 m (5.2–5.7 ft)
Weight:	770–910 kg (1,700–2,000 lbs)
Feed on:	Hay, alfalfa, oat, barley, fresh grass

Many Breeds

There are several breeds of draught horses: Shirehorses are powerfully built, tall animals, standing up to 2 m (6.5 ft) at the shoulder. This breed is believed to have developed from the medieval great horse that was brought to England by William the Conqueror; the Irish draught horse, the national horse of Ireland, is an active and powerful horse. It is an intelligent, gentle and docile animal and easy to work with. It is usually used for hunting and riding and also makes a good competition horse; the Suffolk Punch was developed to plough the heavy clay soil of the counties of Norfolk and Suffolk. Typically chestnut in colour, these horses are popular for their stamina, strength, health and good temperament.

GOATS

Goats were domesticated about 10,000 years ago and continue to be bred in farms across the world. They provide milk, meat, hair and skin.

Nutritious Milk

Like cows, goats are also bred for dairy purposes. The milk can be drunk or processed into cheese. Goats' milk contains less lactose (a type of sugar) than cows' milk so is recommended to those with an intolerance. Unlike cows' milk, goats' milk is naturally homogenised (meaning it stays smooth): this is because it lacks the protein agglutinin.

Goats' milk has comparatively low levels of cholesterol and is extremely rich in phosphorus, calciums and vitamins

CREATURE PROFILE

Common Name:	Angora goat
Weight:	Male: 82-102 kg (180-225 lbs)
	Female: 32-50 kg (70-110 lbs)
Feed on:	Shrubs, bushes and woody plants

Soft Fleece

Some goats are bred for their fibre. Goats wear two coats of hair: an outer coat, which is coarse and is the longer guard hair, and an inner, softer, fleece coat. The latter is used to make soft wool. The fleece is either sheared or combed. Fleece from goats is much more expensive than sheep wool since goats yield a better quality but a lesser amount of fibre. The fleeces of Angora and Cashmere goats are very famous.
They are fine, soft and very warm and often used to make shawls with intricate embroidery.

◀ *Cashmere goats are usually very healthy animals and also require minimal care to raise*

Meat and Hide

The goat is useful both alive and dead. When alive it provides milk and fleece and provides meat and hide when dead. The goat's meat is tender, with low fat content compared to other red meat like beef. It is popular in the Middle East, South Asia, Africa and The West Indies. One of the most popular goats raised for meat is the South African boer. In places like Indonesia goatskin is used to make a native instrumental drum skin named bedug.

▶ *Both the meat and the skin of the goat are used for various purposes*

DONKEYS AND MULES

In some parts of the world mules and donkeys often serve as beasts of burden on farms. They help in transporting heavy loads from one place to another and are also often ridden.

Donkeys

Donkeys have many uses at the farm. They not only function as beasts of burden helping to pull carts and buggies but also make excellent stable companion for foals and horses because of their generally friendly nature. They can also have a calming effect on nervous horses. The miniature Mediterranean donkey is a unique species and is known for its small size. It originates from the island of Sicily. Because of its size, the Mediterranean was traditionally used to turn grinding stones for grain inside people's houses.

Mules

The mule is the offspring of a male donkey and a female horse. It has the patience, endurance and balance of a donkey and the strength and power of a horse. They are also naturally resistant to diseases that many horses suffer from. Mules are supposedly stubborn. However, it is up to the trainer to earn their confidence and make them work.

Despite their reputation, Mules are generally very patient and hardworking animals - although they do have a dangerous kick if provoked

The most common role of a donkey is to be used as transport or to pull carts and heavy loads

CREATURE PROFILE

Common name:	Mediterranean donkey
Colour:	Grey, brown or black with a cross-like pattern on their back
Height:	0.76–0.9 m (2.5–2.95 ft)
Weight:	113–204 kg (250–450 lbs)
Feed on:	Hay and grass

Better than Horses?

Donkeys and mules are typically slower and smaller than horses and are sometimes less powerful. Despite this they are often preferred on farms: they have more endurance; their skin is harder and less sensitive; they suffer fewer problems with their hooves to horses; donkeys and mules are also less choosy about what food they eat and are therefore cheaper to feed; because of their hardiness these animals usually require less care and maintenance than horses.

Donkeys have been used as a mode of transport for many years

SHEEP

Sheep are peaceful animals that can be easily tamed. Man domesticated sheep over 10,000 years ago. Sheep yield wool, sheepskin, excellent meat and even milk.

Sheep Farming

Sheep farming, also known as sheep husbandry, is the raising of sheep for various products. Lambs, or young sheep, are raised for their tender meat while the adults provide us with wool. Some sheep are even raised for milk. Sheep are kept in flocks or a group in pens or barns. They are grazers and need enough field or paddock to graze on. But farmers have to ensure that the paddock is fenced to prevent sheep from wandering away. Coyotes, foxes and wild dogs pose a threat to sheep, particularly newborn lambs. In the case of larger flocks, shepherds and sheep dogs are used to look after and protect the flock.

Warm Wool

Shearing is the process by which the woollen fleece of a sheep is removed. A sheep is typically sheared once a year. The shearer traditionally used a blade shear, but now a machine shear is used for speed and ease of use. Skilled shearers take great pride in the number and quality of fleeces they can shear in a day. In some parts of the world they even hold competitions where shearers compete to prove who is the best!

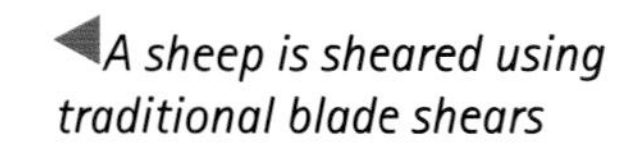

A sheep is sheared using traditional blade shears

CREATURE PROFILE

Common Name:	Southdown sheep
Colour:	Cream, beige and grey with black face and legs
Weight:	Male: 86-104 kg (190-230 lbs)
	Female: 59-81 kg (130-180 lbs)
Feed on:	Hay, legumes, alfalfa

▲*Sheep need large patches of fresh grass to graze on*

Different Breeds

Different breeds of sheep are bred for different purposes. Some yield more wool, some yield more meat, while some female sheep produce more lambs in a year and some others are fast growing. The southdown breed is one of the woolliest sheep breeds of the UK. It yields wool of fine texture and thickness. The Suffolk breed is one of the most dominant mutton sheep breeds in the world, while the east friesian is the most milk productive: it gives between 300-600 litres (80-160 gallons) of milk per year!

▶*The Southdown sheep is known for good lambing ability and produces average quantities of milk*

PIGS

Pigs are also known as hogs or swine. Domestic pigs are usually pink or brown with hair on their bodies. They are bred for their meat.

Pens and Piggeries

Piggeries are animal farms that specialise in rearing domestic pigs for commercial use. In this system of pig production, mature pigs are kept indoors in sheds while pregnant female pigs, also known as sows, are kept in separate stalls. Breeding pigs in piggeries improves the general condition of the pigs. Pigs do not have sweat glands, so most breeds are at risk from heatstroke in hot temperatures. Piggeries control the temperature through ventilation and drip water systems. Pigs produce a lot of waste so it is important that they are frequently mucked-out.

CREATURE PROFILE

Common name:	Domestic pig
Colour:	Mainly brown and black
Weight:	100 kg (220 lbs)
Feed on:	Plants, fungi, roots, grain and berries

Pigs are usually housed together in piggeries

Domestic Pig

The domestic pig is a descendant the wild pig but has a milder temperament. The domestic pig is a pack animal and is usually kept in large groups of 10 animals. The sows are usually more aggressive than the male pigs or boars and are kept separate. The domestic pig is one of the most popular breeds to be reared commercially because its meat is more tender and has a higher fat content than other breeds. Other than for its meat, the domestic pig is also used for its skin and intestines. Even the hair on its skin can be used to make brushes.

▲The domestic pig is reared mainly for its meat, known as pork

England's Own

The large black pig, known as the Devon pig, is the only black pig found in Britain. Originally bred in Devon, these pigs have a shorter body and stronger bones than other breeds. The dark coloured coat makes this breed extremely hardy and also helps prevent skin diseases more common in other pigs. This hardy species also yields good quantity of meat and excellent milk.

▼*Large black pigs, or Devon pigs, are also known for the superior quality of milk that they produce*

DOGS

Some breeds of dog are specially trained for herding animals on farms. Indeed, dogs are a common sight on many farms.

Styles of Work

Herding dogs have physical characteristics like speed and endurance that help them to work. They are used to protect farm animals from wild animals and other threats. Although most commonly used to herd sheep, dogs are sometimes used to control cattle, goats and even poultry, by moving them to the desired spot. Herding dogs are highly trained and responsive to their master's instruction. Signals and commands are usually given in the form of whistles and shouts - each one prompting the dog to act in a different way towards the herd.

The Australian cattle dog is a muscular and strong animal

Grazing sheep are watched closely by the border collie

CREATURE PROFILE

Common Name:	Border collie
Colour:	Mainly black with white patches
Height:	0.4–0.5 m (1.3–1.6 ft)
Weight:	14–23 kg (30–50 lbs)
Feed on:	Ideally, low-fat, high protein meat and biscuits

Australian Cattle Dog

The Australian cattle dog is also known as the Queensland heeler. This medium-sized dog was instrumental in building the cattle industry of Australia. It is alert, courageous and hardy. It is also very cautious by nature. This dog is a nipping dog (meaning it chases the heels of the herd) and is used to move cattle. It is an active breed with excellent stamina and is happiest when involved in some kind of activity or exercise.

Border Collie

The border collie is a popular farm dog. Bred originally in Great Britain, it is regarded as one of the most intelligent farm dogs. It is a quick learner and understands human directions well. It is obedient and therefore makes a good farm dog. With its great energy, agility and herding instincts it can manage many kinds of animals – from sheep and cattle to poultry. This dog is a header dog, meaning it will run ahead (and around) the herd in order to affect its movements.

A border collie prepares to 'come by' - an instruction given to it by the herder

CHICKENS

Chickens are the most common and widespread domesticated animal in the world. They are usually mass-bred for meat and to produce eggs, but are also commonly kept as pets in some parts of the world.

Cluck Cluck!

Male chickens are known as roosters while female chickens are called hens. Chickens are gregarious (social) birds and live in large flocks. Chickens like to lay eggs in nests that already contain eggs - something that is often encouraged by farmers with the placing of fake eggs. Domestic chickens cannot fly long distances, but those raised in open-air farms generally have the feathers of one of their wings clipped to prevent them from flying over boundary fences.

Cornish Hens

The Cornish hen is widely bred for the poultry meat industry. They were first bred in the county of Cornwall in England and were known for their large amount of white meat and smooth and fine texture. They have short feathers, stuck closely to their body. These birds need adequate shelter during winter, as their feathers do not provide enough insulation to keep them warm.

▼*Chicken is one of the most commonly used meats in the world and most parts of the bird can be used as food*

Roman Dorkings

It is believed that the dorking breed of chicken was originally bred in Italy during the reign of Julius Caesar. It was later introduced to England, where the breed was reared commercially. It is considered to be the purest breed because of the five claws on its foot, rather than the usual four. The dorking chicken is a very hardy bird and is extremely active, requiring plenty of space to roam. It is reared both for its meat and eggs and is known to lay eggs in the early part of the year. This bird takes up to two years to grow to a size suitable to eat and can live up to seven years of age. It needs to be given good quality feed to achieve a good weight and size.

▶The dorking chickens are foraging birds and require a large amount of space to move around in

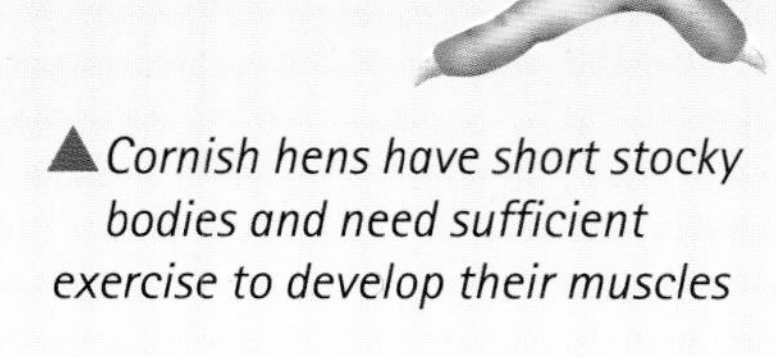

▲Cornish hens have short stocky bodies and need sufficient exercise to develop their muscles

CREATURE PROFILE

Common Name:	Dorking
Colour:	Silver-grey, dark red or white
Weight:	Male: 4 kg (9 lbs)
	Female: 2.7 kg (6 lbs)
Feed on:	Grain, grass and insects

TURKEYS

The turkey is a large bird, found originally in the forests of North America. Today it is bred commercially on farms around the world and is best associated with Christmas celebrations.

Turkey Types

There are two main species of turkeys – the Wild turkey and the Ocellated turkey. Wild turkeys are good fliers and also relatively cunning birds. They are identified by an almost featherless bluish head with a striking red throat in the males. The head also has fleshy growths called caruncles. Wild turkeys live in woodland, where their extremely sharp eyesight allows them to spot danger and adopt a quick means of escape. In the wild, turkeys may nest at the base of a tree during the day, but by night they move higher up and roost in the branches.

Wild turkeys have a very striking appearance with a particularly dense plumage

Turkey Treat

The domesticated turkey is raised commercially for its meat and is a descendant of the wild turkey. It is reared extensively in temperate parts of the world. Modern techniques in farming, coupled with a high seasonal demand, have made turkey farming a large-scale operation; the bird is most commonly associated with Christmas celebrations as being a bird large enough to feed gathered families. The most widely-bred variety of domesticated turkey is the broad-breasted white, which is known for its high yield of breast meat, but is said by some to hold less flavour as a result.

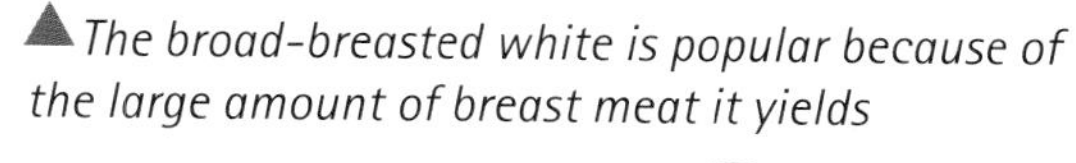

The broad-breasted white is popular because of the large amount of breast meat it yields

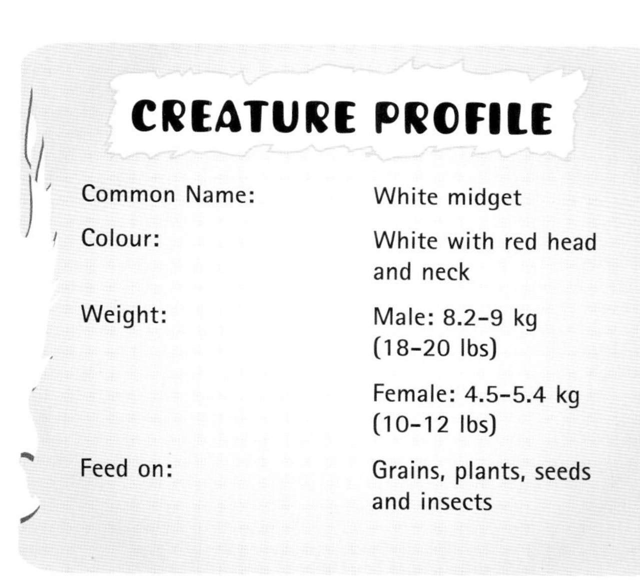

CREATURE PROFILE

Common Name:	White midget
Colour:	White with red head and neck
Weight:	Male: 8.2-9 kg (18-20 lbs)
	Female: 4.5-5.4 kg (10-12 lbs)
Feed on:	Grains, plants, seeds and insects

Raising Turkeys

Traditionally, turkeys were bred for their meat during Christmas. Now, they are produced through the year on a large scale. They are reared in large sheds or in barns. Turkeys reared for meat are usually hatched by artificial means. Most commonly turkey hens are now artificially inseminated to fertilise their eggs, as the physical development of male turkeys largely makes them incapable of breeding.

Using artificial incubators to hatch eggs allows breeders to control the number of birds and rear them according to demand

DUCKS

Ducks are common water birds. Many species of ducks are raised on farms for eggs, meat and their soft feathers. Most domestic species of ducks have been bred from the wild mallard duck.

Pekin Duck

Donald duck, the famous fictional character, is a pekin duck. The classic white pekin duck is a very popular duck breed on farms. It is quite hardy and has a mild temperament and is easy to train, domesticate and pet. It is a fast growing duck and also an excellent egg-layer, laying up to 200 eggs a year. But female pekin ducks are not good brooders, so the eggs usually need to be incubated artificially. The pekin duck is very popular as a meat duck. Adult pekin ducks are white in colour and have orange-yellow bills, legs and feet. The hatchlings have bright yellow-coloured plumage with orange feet.

Rouen Duck

The rouen closely resembles its ancestor, the wild mallard. It is marked with similar colour patterns with a green head, white collar, claret breast and bright-blue feathers on its wings. It is a heavy duck and can weigh up to 5.5 kg (12 lbs). It is not a good egg-layer, typically laying only 100 eggs a year. However, it does yield a good quantity of meat known for its great flavour and is popular for this across Europe. It is used mainy as a roasting duck.

Unlike the brightly-coloured male rouen, the female is distinguished by warm brown colours

Muscovy

The muscovy is another large farm duck. It is the only domestic duck that has not been bred from the mallard duck. It has a bright red crest around its eyes, above the beak. Its feet are equipped with strong and sharp claws that help the bird to roost. It prefers to fly rather than swim. These birds are average egg layers, laying about 80-90 eggs every year. Their meat is leaner than most breeds of duck.

CREATURE PROFILE

Common Name:	Pekin duck
Colour:	White
Weight:	3.5–5 kg (8–11 lbs)
Length:	About 75 cm (30 in)
Feed on:	Insects, grasses and plants

▲ *The muscovy duck has a dark coloured body with white wings and long talons on its feet*

▼ *The pekin duck has relatively weak legs and feet meaning it prefers to swim rather than walk around the farm*

OTHER LIVESTOCK

Apart from cattle, horses, sheep, pigs and poultry, some farms also rear more unusual animals like elk, llama, bison and ostrich for commercial purposes; their meat and other products are becoming increasingly accepted.

Elk

The elk is a member of the deer family. It is bred mainly for its antlers and also for game hunting. The antlers of the elk are used to make medicines in South Korea. The male elk has antlers, which are shed every year. The weight of the antlers increases year on year: a one-year-old elk's antlers typically weigh 1.3 kg (2.8 lbs), while a full-grown adult's might weigh up to 11kg (24 lbs).

▼*Alpacas are social animals and live in herds usually at higher altitudes*

◀*The elk is the second largest species of deer in the world*

Llama and Alpaca

The llama and alpaca both belong to the camel family. The llama resembles a camel but lacks a hump while the alpaca looks like a large sheep. The llama often serves as a beast of burden in some parts of the world, carrying loads from one place to another, especially in hilly areas. Its thick and leathery hoof pads help it get a grip of the rocky surface where most other animals would stumble. The alpaca is bred for its fine wool. Its fleece produces wool, which is much softer and lighter than the wool obtained from sheep. Moreover, the alpaca yields white wool, which is easy to dye in various shades.

CREATURE PROFILE

Common name:	Llama
Colour:	Creamy-white, grey, brown, red or black, or a combination thereof
Height:	1.6–1.8 m (5.5–6 ft) at the shoulder
Weight:	102–204 kg (225–450 lbs)
Feed on:	Shrubs, grass, leaves, lichen

Ostrich

The first South African ostrich farm was founded in 1838. Today ostrich farming is a very profitable enterprise. Most ostrich farms are found in South Africa even today. The ostriches are bred and raised commercially for their meat, skin and feathers. Ostriches yield red meat that tastes like beef and is a delicacy among food lovers. Ostrich leather is very soft and is used to make shoes and bags. The feathers are used to clean fine machinery and even as fashion accessories.

▼*Ostrich meat is slowly gaining popularity in the world because it is low in fat and cholesterol*

TAKING CARE

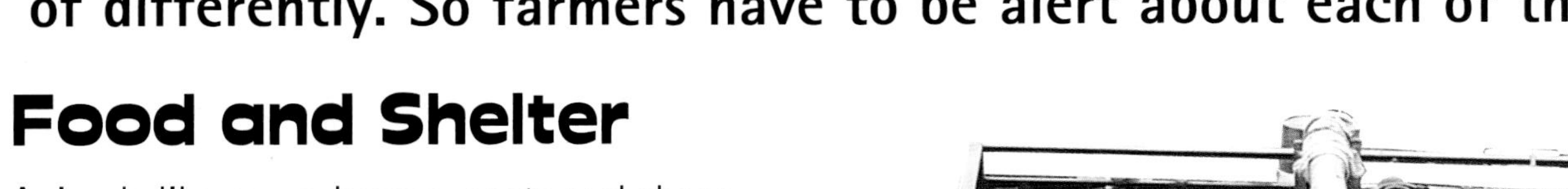

Animals at the farm need proper feed, care and medication to stay healthy. Every animal has a different diet and needs to be taken care of differently. So farmers have to be alert about each of their needs.

Food and Shelter

Animals like cows, horses, goats and sheep are all plant eaters but they eat different kinds of plants. The diet of particular animals can depend on the work they do on the farm. Draught horses need more concentrates than the amount needed for cows. Pregnant animals also need a special diet to produce healthy babies. Animals like cows, horses and goats are kept in barns or stables while pigs and sheep are sometimes kept in pens. Farmers must ensure that the barns and pens are spacious, airy, safe and clean. This will help the farm animals stay healthy and happy.

▶*In many parts of the world there are strict guidelines governing how animals are transported*

Handling Tricks

Handling facilities for cattle and other farm animals do not have to be elaborate and expensive but should be safe and well-controlled. Regular cleaning and maintenance of all kinds of equipment used at the farm is important to avoid any chance of disease or infection. Cattle sorting, loading and transporting is a very important aspect of commercial farming. All vehicles used should have a proper flooring, solid latches and adequate ventilation to allow the animals to move about and breathe freely in the vehicle during transportation.

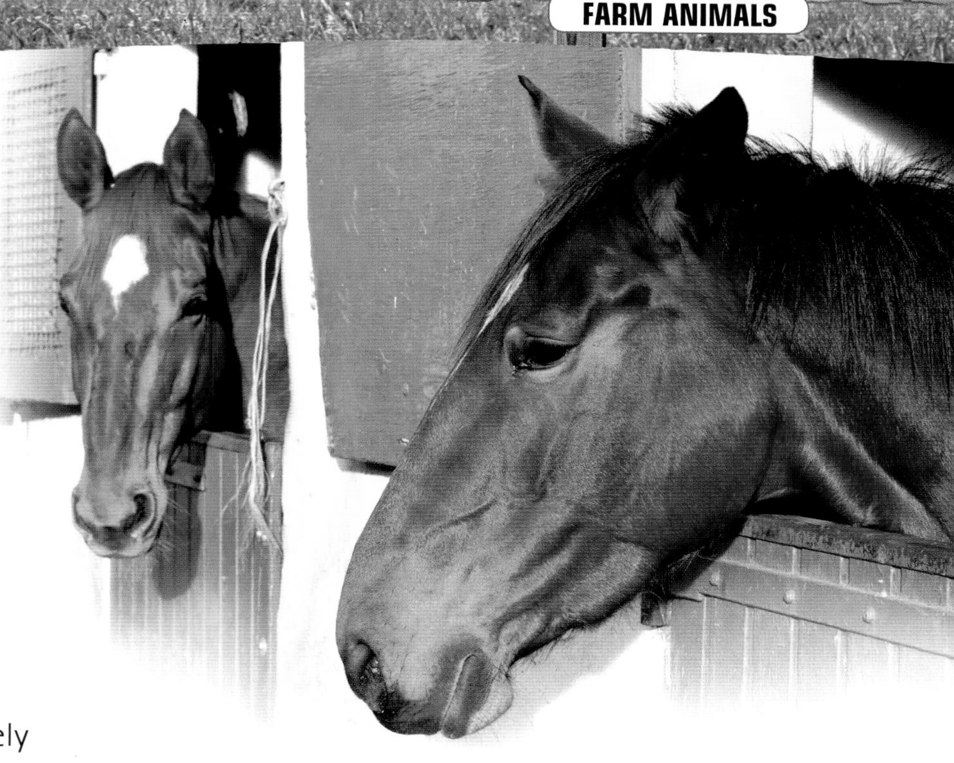

▲*Stables and barns need to be kept clean to avoid disease and infection*

▼*Farm animals need to be checked regularly for symptoms of diseases and given proper medical treatment*

Disease and Cure

Animals at the farm are prone to illness. Because many animals live together on farms in concentration, the threat of infections spreading is a real and present danger: flu is a common threat to many farm animals; bluetongue, a viral disease in cattle, goats and sheep causes inflammation and swelling of mouth, nose and tongue and can be fatal if not treated; cloven-hooved animals are at particual risk of foot problems and must be shoed regularly to avoid diseases like laminitis and even lameness. Hygienic conditions and healthy living help prevent diseases.

POULTRY CARE

▲*Poultry coops should be clean, hygienic and safe from predators and other farm animals*

The health of poultry affects their eggs and meat, so proper feed and medication is important. Poultry also face the threat of predation from other animals, so measures need to be taken for their protection.

Home Sweet Home

Having clean and safe housing for poultry is of the utmost importance. Some farms let their poultry run free. This gives the poultry freedom but might be dangerous and lead to accidents and fatalities. Farms can also opt for a bottomless poultry coop which can be transferred from one place to the other on the farm; this keeps them safe while allowing them enough freedom to move within the coop. Poultry coops do not need to be very elaborate but should fulfill basic requirements by providing proper ventilation and shelter.

Caring for the Young

Looking after young chicks and ducklings is a very important part of poultry care. Both the young and the parent need to be provided food and water separately. Often the mother breaks the grain into smaller pieces in order to feed her young. The food should be in a container that cannot be tipped over by the chicks or ducklings while feeding. The water should also be kept in a shallow container so that the chicks do not drown. The young birds should be moved to a larger rearing coop when they are about 8 weeks of age.

Common Diseases

Bird flu is a common yet potentially dangerous disease. Not only does it spread rapidly, but, if not detected properly it can also affect the health of anybody who might eat the meat. Precaution and medical attention can, however, reduce its threat. Fowl cholera, fowl typhoid and fowl pox are other common diseases in poultry. Most of these diseases can be prevented by a healthy diet. Poultry feed should ideally contain 20-22 per cent of proteins with coccodiostat, a chemical that helps to build immunity. Cleanliness and hygiene also helps prevent most poultry diseases.

▲*All poultry should be given a separate place and dish for their food and water and the parent and young should be fed separately*

▼*For the first weeks after birth, the chicks should be kept with their parent*

Learn to care for your
horse or pony!
Horse &
Pony Care

Understanding Your Horse or Pony

It is not enough to just have a pet horse or pony. You must take proper care to ensure your animal's comfort and health.

Establish a bond of love and trust with your pet

Top Tips

It is a good idea to let your horse or pony smell your hand so that they recognise your scent. They will become familiar with you this way.

First Things First

Your horse or pony neither know you or their new surroundings. So you must first try to form a bond with them. Communicate with them as much as possible and try to understand them. Be affectionate and gentle. Be reassuring so that they can trust you. Do not force them to do things they do not want to. Do not be too tough with them. Remember being a master does not mean that you can bully your pet. Show them around their new home so that they get familiar with their new surrounding. Take extra effort to make them feel protected and cared for.

To Show you Care

Your responsibility as a master does not end after you bond with your horse or pony. In fact it only begins there. Your horse or pony's health depends on diet, exercise and cleanliness. So you must take good care of what you feed them. You have to find time to take them out for exercise. Keeping them clean is extremely important too. And do not forget to clean their stable. Remember that a hygienic surrounding is the key to good health for everybody.

The stable is the home for your horse or pony. Remember to design it in a way that is safe and comfortable for them - a place where they would like to stay.

Home Sweet Home

You can make a ready-to-assemble wooden stable or one with bricks. The latter is stronger and safer too. The stable should be airy and roomy. Since horses are bigger they need more space and larger stables than ponies. There should be enough natural light available during the day. It should have an accessible water supply and proper drainage system. Concrete floors are easier to clean so they should be preferred. Straw, paper or Auboise beds can be used as bedding for your horse or pony. The stable should have buckets, hay nets, mangers, as well as tying rings for them. Separate food storage space and tack rooms are important too.

Horses and ponies need clean, safe and comfortable living quarters

Take all necessary precautions to prevent fire in the stable

Safe and Secure

The stable must be safe for your horse or pony. Remember, prevention is better than cure so make sure all electrical fittings are safe with circuit breakers. Hay catches fire easily so store it in a separate space. Keep fire extinguishers in the stable. It is best to have at least two exits out of the stable. To prevent thefts you can put a burglar alarm in the tack room.

Muck breeds disease and must be cleared out daily

Store all the equipment you need to clean the stable in a proper place

Cleanliness is Next to Godliness

The stable should be clean and germ free as dirty stables breed disease. You must muck out every morning: for this you need a wheelbarrow, a shovel, a rake, a fork or shavings scoop, broom, skip or bucket, hose and gloves. Tie the horse or pony outside the stable before you begin cleaning. Clean the bedding as well as the floor and put the muck heap well away from the stable. You must use traps or poison to control rats and mice as they cause damage and spread disease too.

Top Tips

Take every possible care to make sure that the stable for your horse or pony is a safe place for them, do not forget to get your stable insured so that you are reimbursed in case of any accident.

Feeding Well

What you feed your horse or pony determines their wellbeing. They need different types of food to stay healthy and work well. It is important to make sure that they are not eating the same type of food for every meal.

Roughage

Horses and ponies graze on grass in their natural surrounding. However, stabled horses and ponies are fed hay. Hay is the main source of roughage, which is important for their digestive system. It helps to add bulk to the food and is filling. You must feed them good quality hay. Good hay is greenish-brown, sweet smelling and shakes out freely. On average, your horse or pony's diet should contain about 70 per cent roughage.

Horses and ponies enjoy feeding on good hay

Concentrates

Apart from hay, your horse or pony needs other nutritious food. These are concentrates - food that give energy for physical labour. Concentrates include oats and barley. Oats can be crushed and fed raw while barley is best fed boiled as it is easily digested in that form. You can even buy concentrate feeds ready-mixed that are suitable for your breed of horse or pony. Concentrates should be about 25-30 per cent of their diet. Avoid feeding concentrates if your horse or pony is at rest, because then the diet can prove too rich for them.

Crushed oats are the best source of concentrates for horses and ponies

Supplements

Stabled horses and ponies need some fresh produce in their diet too. You can either allow them to graze on grass for 10-15 minutes everyday or supplement their diet with fruit and vegetables like apples and carrots. You can feed them yourself to your horse or pony as treats when they behave well. Make sure that you slice them thin, lengthways to avoid any possibility of choking. Fresh food provides your horse or pony with vitamins and minerals that are important for their overall health.

Fruits and vegetables fed in small quantities are good for the overall health of horses and ponies

Top Tips

Horses and ponies need water along with their food. Water not only quenches thirst but helps in digestion too. Make sure to keep adequate fresh water for them in buckets in the stable at all times. Make sure they have access to water if they are grazing outside.

Diet and Routine

In their natural habitat horses and ponies graze over a large area and feed little, but often. When stabled, however, their diet and routine are changed.

How Much and When?

The quantity and quality of feed depend on your horse or pony's size and the kind of work they do. Both under-fed and over-fed horses and ponies will not keep in good health. It is best to know your horse or pony's weight and feed them accordingly. They are usually fed about two percent of their body weight, most of which is roughage. Stabled horses and ponies should be fed twice or thrice in a day and always at the same time.

Things to Remember

- *Do not over-feed or under-feed your horse or pony*
- *Always feed good quality food*
- *Remember to keep food and water buckets clean*
- *Never feed your horse or pony just before or after exercise*
- *Let them graze on fresh grass occasionally*
- *Remember to add fruit and vegetables in their diet*
- *Prevent them from drinking too much water immediately after feeding or exercise*
- *Feed them from your hand to show that you care*

Horse and Pony Portions

Since horses are bigger they need more food than ponies. Moreover, ponies have a tendency to gain weight so you must maintain a strict diet for them. Horses generally require more energy-giving concentrates as they work more. Ponies run the risk of foundering much more than horses and should never be fed grain. Bran or husks of wheatgrain are a good alternative for grain and can be fed to both horses and ponies.

Hay can be put in clean buckets or hay nets

Note the difference in size of a horse (right) and pony (left). Being bigger, horses need more feed

Common Questions

Where should I store the food?

You should store your horse or pony's food in a dry place in the stable to keep it fresh. But remember to store it away from the pony!

Pasture Management

Horses and ponies are happiest when they are grazing out on fields. Pastures not only provide the necessary forage that they need but also provide a good exercise area.

Taking Care of Grazing Land

Managing the pasture well is of utmost importance. It requires a lot of time and effort but yields rewards for your horse or pony, as well as you. You need to choose the grass that suits the soil type as well as your horse or pony. They are fond of legumes , so plant some. Use good fertilizers and make sure that you weed the field regularly. Remove droppings to prevent the grass from becoming sour. This also checks the breeding of diseases. Rotating the grazing land replenishes the soil, interrupts the worms' life cycle and reduces infestation.

Fresh, green, juicy grass is every horse and pony's favourite meal!

Fences should be at a height that horses and ponies cannot jump over

Boundaries and Fences

The boundaries of a pasture help to control how much of the paddock your horse and pony have access to. It is best to divide the grazing into at least two sections. Your horse or pony can have access to one paddock while the other can be rested. The fence enclosing your land stops any stray animal from entering or grazing in your field. You must choose the fencing that is safest for your horse or pony. The best option is fence posts and rail fencing, which is usually made of wood. Electric fencing and hedges are the other options. Barbed wire is very dangerous and should never be used.

Shelter and Water

When your horse or pony is turned out to graze, it will need shelter to protect itself from the scorching sun and rain. You can either have a building with a roof in the field or plant lots of trees in the centre of the field to provide natural shelter. Ensuring sufficient water supply is extremely important. Keep a large trough and remember to change the water every day. This is in addition to the water you keep in the stable.

Top Tips

When grass is in abundance, horses and ponies tend to put on weight and run the risk of foundering. Therefore, it is essential to restrict their grazing. It will help if they exercise, but do not make them exercise hard soon after a meal.

A shelter in the pasture is a must for horses and ponies

Turning Out Horses and Ponies

After you have a good pasture for your horse or pony you need to learn the art of turning them out in the field to graze.

Controlling the Excitement

Most horses and ponies love the prospect of grazing. They get so excited that they tend to run off, dragging you along too! You need to learn to control them to avoid any accident. Use a long lead rope to lead out, as it is easier to control them with that. Avoid turning out over-enthusiastic horses and ponies at the same time every day so that they do not wait in anticipation. You could try giving them a tit-bit so that they wait for it before they run off. If nothing works then simply ride to the paddock, dismount and remove the tack.

Shy Horses and Ponies

Some horses and ponies on the other hand are shy and you may face a difficulty in turning them out. They avoid going out because they are scared. You should try to dispel their fears. Introduce them to the pasture slowly. Keep them where they can see the open field so that they get familiar with it. Put some hay and water in the paddock, take them there, talk to them to reassure them, leave them for a few minutes and fetch them back. They will begin to associate the paddock with food. Then increase the time gradually.

TopTips

Remember to wear gloves when you turn out your horse or pony. This will prevent rope burn or cuts in case they pull the rope hard. Remember never to wrap the rope around your hand because, should they run suddenly, you might be dragged along.

Turning out horses and ponies is an art to be learnt!

Things to Remember

- *Use enough fly spray on your horse or pony especially during summer, to save them from the nuisance of pests*
- *Cover your horse or pony with a warm blanket when your turn them out in winter*
- *Limit their grazing time to prevent over feeding*
- *Make the pasture a safe place for them with fresh grass free from poisonous weeds, and safe fence and boundary*
- *When you offer a tit-bit be careful how you hold it, as there might be a chance of an enthusiastic horse or pony struggling to get it and hurting you accidentally*
- *Stand beside them when you lead them out and neither pull the rope too hard, nor let it slack - be firm*

It is best to have a stable that overlooks a pasture

The Grooming Kit

Did you know that special brushes are available for grooming or cleaning your horse or pony? These brushes are kept together in a plastic box or canvas bag. This is known as the grooming kit.

Grooming Kit List

- *Rubber curry comb: It is used to remove dried mud and loose hair from the pony*
- *Dandy brush: A brush with stiff bristles used to remove dried mud and dirt from the legs*
- *Body brush: It has soft bristles and can be used on the entire body to remove dirt*
- *Metal curry comb: It is used to remove dirt off the body brush during grooming*
- *Mane comb: Plastic or metal combs used to brush the mane and tail*
- *Hoof pick: Usually metal, used for removing dirt and stones from the hooves*
- *Sponges: One for cleaning eyes and nose and the other for the dock area*
- *Sweat scraper: It is used to wipe excess sweat or water off*
- *Linen: A good linen drying-up cloth can be dampened and gently wiped over the body to give it a final polish*

A body brush, gently rubbed, leaves your horse or pony's body shining

A nicely groomed horse looks smart and healthy

Top Tips

Always ensure that you keep all grooming equipment clean. Remove hair from brushes and combs and always clean the sponge after every use. Anything dirty in your grooming kit could lead to a skin disease for your horse or pony.

Keeping Clean

Just as you wash to keep yourself clean, your horse or pony must be kept clean too. Grooming is a very important part of horse and pony care, and must be done very regularly.

Importance of Grooming

Grooming helps to keep your horse or pony neat and tidy. It keeps their coat shiny and makes them look smart. It also helps to keep your horse or pony free from lice. Grooming gently massages your horse or pony, helps to increase blood circulation and builds their muscles. When you groom your horse or pony you can always check carefully for any wounds or sores that it may have and treat them immediately. Grooming also helps to build a good relationship with your horse or pony and shows that you care.

How Often Should I Groom?

You should groom your horse or pony every day, as it gets dirty after exercise. Even if you do not take the horse or pony out for exercise one day, you should not skip grooming. Bathe your horse or pony using good shampoos meant for them. But do that only when it is absolutely essential. Remember to wash them only when the weather is warm. While giving them a bath, do not splash the water all in one go - sprinkle a little water at a time. Use the sweat scraper to wipe off the water, or they might catch a cold. But not giving them a bath does not mean that you skip the grooming. That is absolutely essential. Remember to give your horse or pony a brisk rubdown soon after it has done vigorous exercise, so that the sweat does not stay on the skin.

Dirt and mud must be rubbed off the horse or pony's body with care

Common Questions

Why shouldn't horses and ponies be bathed regularly?

Bathing removes the natural oils from your horse or pony's skin. These oils protect the skin against dirt and even cold. Soaking the coat tends to wash these oils away making your horse or pony vulnerable.

Things to Remember

- *Always tie your pony safely before you begin grooming*
- *Begin grooming at the shoulder and go up the neck so that your pony knows where you are. Stroke the rubber curry comb firmly, but gently, in the direction of the hair to remove the dirt. Use circular movements to bring out loose hair*
- *Pick up the Dandy brush and go down the front legs. Be careful! Do not put your face in front of the legs. You may get a knee in your face if your animal picks its leg up suddenly*
- *Now move towards its barrel, its quarters and its hind legs. Stand close to its quarters while cleaning its hind legs to avoid a kick*
- *When brushing its face, start from the side so that the animal does not feel scared. Rub off the dirt as gently as possible*
- *After dried mud and dirt has been removed, use the body brush gently to produce a shine*
- *Do not forget to brush the mane, preferably with a plastic mane brush. Always comb in the direction of hair*
- *Comb your animal's tail similarly*
- *Use a damp sponge to gently clean your animal's eyes, nose and dock area*
- *For an extra smart look, perhaps before a show, apply some coat gloss and rub off gently*

Make sure that the horse or pony does not feel scared when bathed

Of Manes and Tails

A thick and shiny mane and tail add to your horse or pony's beauty. However, if they are unkempt, they can make your horse or pony look very untidy.

Combing

Always use plastic and not metal combs for your horse or pony. Brush down in sections to remove the tangles. Do not pull too hard. While combing the tail, stand to one side and pull the tail gently towards you to avoid an accidental kick from your horse or pony. You can use a grooming spray that helps to detangle the hair easily.

Washing

Manes and tails tend to get dirty and greasy. It becomes essential to wash them at such times. Remember to wash them only when the weather is warm. Dampen the mane and tail in lukewarm water and then wash with a good quality shampoo. Make sure that the shampoo does not get into your horse or pony's eyes, ears or nose. Rinse off the shampoo and dry with a towel. You can swing the tail to remove excess water. Do it gently. Do not forget to brush the mane and the tail after a wash.

Many horse and pony owners spend a lot of time in beautifying their horse or pony's mane and tail

'Pulling' Manes and Tails

Most horses and ponies have thick manes and tails that can get unmanageable. It is for this reason that manes and tails need to be 'pulled' or thinned. It is best to pull the mane and tail after exercise as the pores are open at this time and excess hair comes out easily. Remove tangles from the hair then wind a few hairs at a time around the comb and pull sharply downwards. Work on it until it looks neat. Remember to pull only a small area every day and work over a week or two for a tidy look.

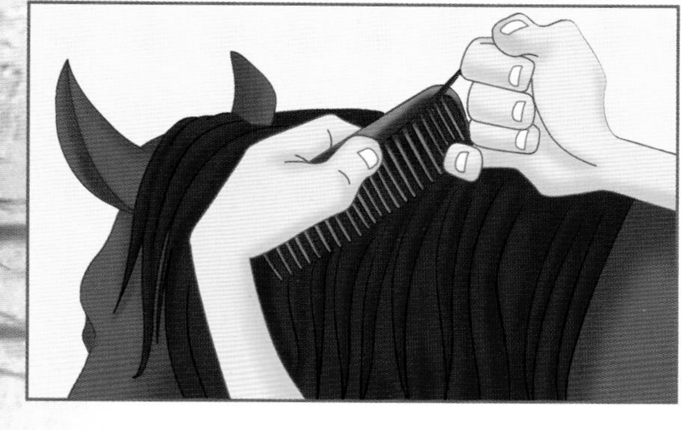

The illustration shows how manes and tails are to be pulled

Common Questions

Can't I just cut my pony's mane and tail?

Never use scissors or clippers to cut your horse or pony's mane and tail. Cutting or trimming can ruin their appearance and make them appear even thicker.

Horse and pony manes can be thinned for their comfort especially during summers

Hoof Care

Your horse or pony's feet need a lot of special care as they rely on their feet to do all the work.

My Shoes are the Best!

Horses and ponies began wearing shoes hundreds of years back when man domesticated them. Shoes protect their hooves when they travel long distances at great speed and carry loads. Nowadays, several types of shoes are available for your horse or pony. Shoes, such as egg-bar or straight-bar, are specially designed to correct any particular foot problem that your horse or pony may have. Fuller shoes are most commonly used for horses and ponies. Extra-grip shoes can be used on horses and ponies that work hard especially on hilly roads or compete on slippery grass.

Shoeing

Your horse and pony must wear properly fitted shoes. For this they need to be shod every six to eight weeks. Regular shoeing prevents disease and lameness among horses and ponies. You must contact a farrier to shoe your horse and pony. He will trim the hooves and shape the shoes to ensure that the shoes are comfortable for them. He will also be able to offer corrective shoeing if that is necessary, so that over the time your horse and pony's feet become healthier. If a shoe comes off for some reason, you must get it replaced immediately.

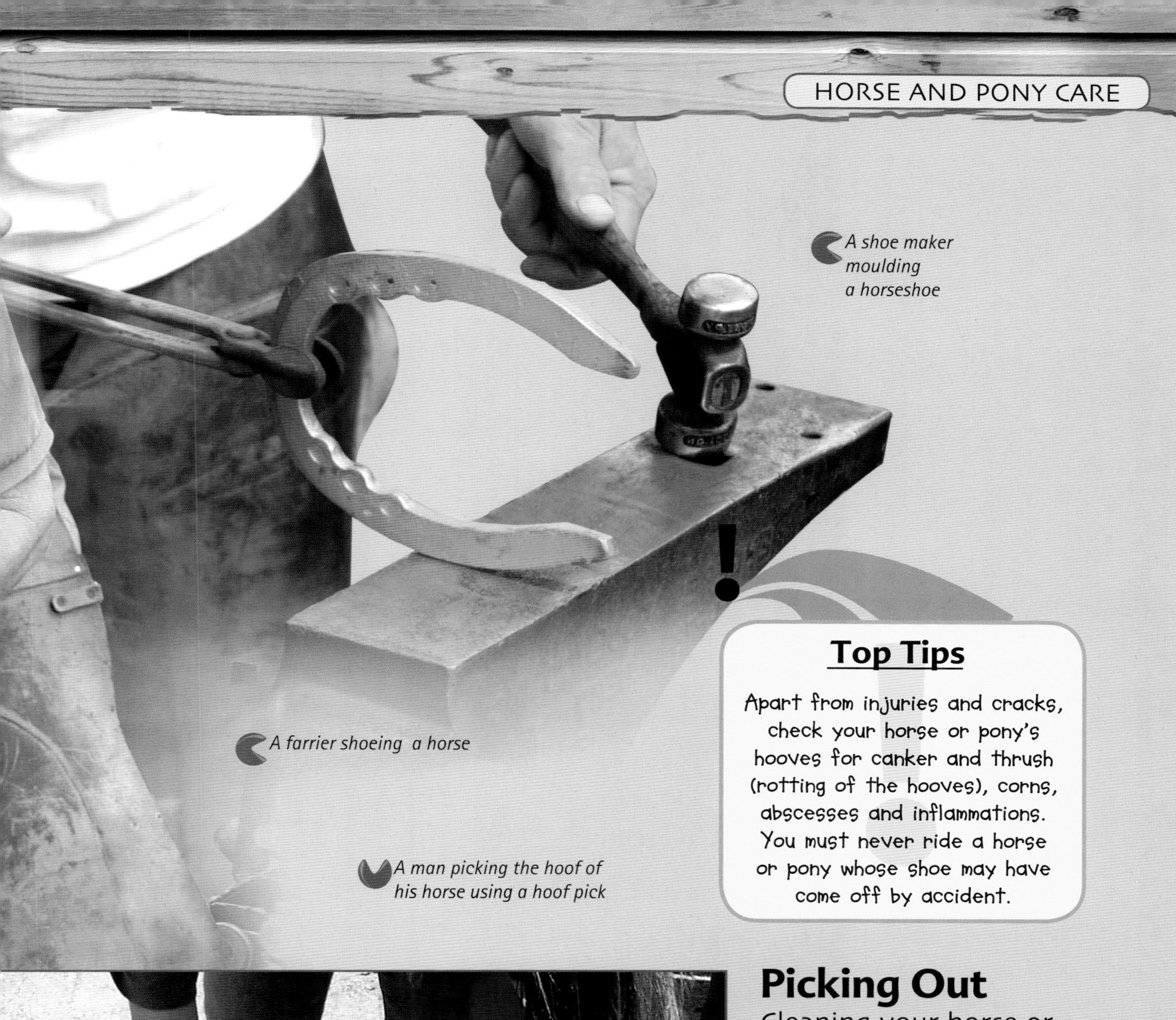

A shoe maker moulding a horseshoe

A farrier shoeing a horse

A man picking the hoof of his horse using a hoof pick

Top Tips

Apart from injuries and cracks, check your horse or pony's hooves for canker and thrush (rotting of the hooves), corns, abscesses and inflammations. You must never ride a horse or pony whose shoe may have come off by accident.

Picking Out

Cleaning your horse or pony's hooves daily is very important. Hold your horse or pony's feet up gently, check the hoof and use the hoof pick to pick out dirt, pebbles or anything else stuck in the sole of the foot. Remember to check for any injury, infection or cracks and consult your farrier in case of any problem. Repeat the process for all four feet.

Keeping Fit

Exercise keeps your horse or pony healthy and fit. Horses and ponies are built for life on the move so you must exercise them every day, except when they are ill.

Since you stand in the middle and instruct your horse or pony, lunging teaches it to pay attention to you

Beginning with the Basics

Tack up your horse or pony before exercise. Do not forget to wear proper gear yourself. Now sit up straight on the saddle, keeping your knees bent and heels down. Relax your arms when you hold the reins. It is a good idea to stretch yourself a bit before you mount your horse or pony. Now begin the exercise of riding by walking them. Instead of a full riding exercise every day, you can occasionally lunge them in a circle around you, remembering to change the direction regularly. This allows the horse or pony to exercise without having to carry extra weight.

On the move

Always begin your horse or pony's exercises with warm-up walks and increase the workload gradually. Encourage them to keep steady as they walk by giving them proper riding aids or signals. A walk should ideally last about 20 minutes after which you can trot them. Build up the pace gradually. Short periods of galloping help to build their stamina. But do not overburden them. Allow them to cool off after fast exercise by walking them slowly. A combination of walk, trot and gallop is the best exercise for your horse or pony, but keep the gallop to a minimum.

Good Riding

Try to supply as many movements to your horse or pony as possible. Make it move in circles and serpentine ways. Walking on roads makes their tendons and muscles stronger, but you must ensure that your horse or pony is comfortable moving on roads and you are well versed in road safety procedures. Do not exercise your horse or pony immediately after a feed or shot. Their hooves must be picked before and after every ride. Just as you enjoy Sundays, give your horse and pony a rest day too.

Take all road safety precautions when you ride on the road

Good riding is that which is comfortable for both you and your horse or pony

Common Questions

What is the Pony Express?

The Pony Express was a mail system that began in April 1960 in old western America where the riders rode without rest to deliver mail. It was the fastest mail system of that time till telegraph was introduced a year later in November. Predictably, the horses that were made to work so hard fell ill and lived only a quarter as long as normal horses.

Summer Care

Summer heat can be hard on your horse or pony. Some basic attention can ensure their comfort and health in the warm weather.

Along the neck

Along the withers

Clipping

Horses and ponies tend to grow more hair in winter. The thick coat can be troublesome in the warm weather so you need to clip or shear them. Clipping will ensure that they cool down quickly after exercise and riding. Depending on your horse or pony's workload, you can choose the type of clip you want. It is advisable to take professional help for clipping your horse and pony.

What a Nuisance!

Flies and mosquitoes are common in summer. They are not just a bother but also breed diseases, so you need to protect your horse against them. The use of fly blankets and sprays helps to reduce these pests. Be careful not to spray in your horse or pony's eyes, nose or mouth. Keep muck heaps well away from the stable to reduce flies.

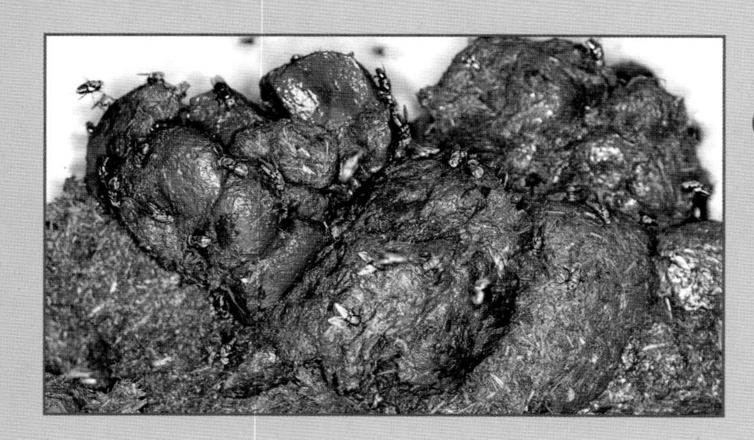

Flies breeding on manure can carry many diseases

The image shows a clipped horse. This is called the hunter clip where hair is left intact around the saddle area and the legs

Crease down the loin

Tailhead

Ribs

Behind the shoulder

Common Questions

What are the various clips for horses and ponies?

The blanket clip, hunter clip, full clip, trace clip and belly and gullet clip are the various options in clipping.

Things to Remember

- *Keep enough fresh water for your horse or pony to drink*
- *You may reduce its diet a little and feed it at cooler hours of the day*
- *Use sun block, especially for grey horses and ponies, to prevent sunburn*
- *Give them some salt as there is a chance of dehydration*
- *If fresh grass is not available, feed them alfalfa, as they need green food in summers*
- *Hang a fan in the stable in a safe position to cool it off*
- *Sponge the horse or pony during excessive heat*

A clipper used to shave the horse or pony

Keeping Warm

Domestic horses and ponies are dependent on us for keeping them warm and protecting them against freezing winters. You have to be careful to do this to avoid any serious illness.

A warm rug is a must during winters as it keeps the horse or pony cozy

I am Cozy

Several types of rugs are available for your horse or pony's comfort. Choose rugs made from natural fibres like wool and jute. Synthetic rugs lined with cotton are easier to clean, so some people prefer them. Night rugs should be thick and warm. Rugs you use during the day should be thinner. Special exercise rugs are used when you take your horse or pony for exercise or a ride in winters. These are placed under the saddle. Rugs usually have cross-over straps. Make sure that you do not tie them too tight, and that the horse or pony is able to breathe easily.

Cleaning the Rugs

Just as you clean your jackets and quilts, your horse or pony's rugs need to be cleaned too. For this you must ensure that you have at least one spare night and day rug that you can use while you wash the first one. Rugs are best cleaned in a washing machine. Remember to follow the manufacturer's washing instructions when you clean the rugs. After the grease and dirt has been removed from the rugs, rinse them and hang them out to dry.

Winter Care

Wild horses and ponies develop natural protection against winter. However, stabled horses and ponies need special attention. Apart from using rugs to keep them warm, their hooves need to be checked thoroughly in winters. If you are riding out, avoid icy and frozen ground and try to limit yourself to walking the horse or pony. Carry a hoof pick and stop periodically to pick out the ice from its soles. Brush your horse and pony often as it provides insulation. Feed them more hay for extra calories that will keep them warm. Remember to keep the drinking water warm. Or they may not want to drink it even when they should.

Top Tips

Regular de-worming is essential in winter as equine parasites are difficult to kill in cold weather. Consult your veterinarian for de-worming doses.

Horses and ponies must be ridden at a slow speed on snow

Tack Care

You need some basic equipment and accessories when you ride your horse or pony. This is known as tack. Tack helps you sit comfortably and control your horse or pony well.

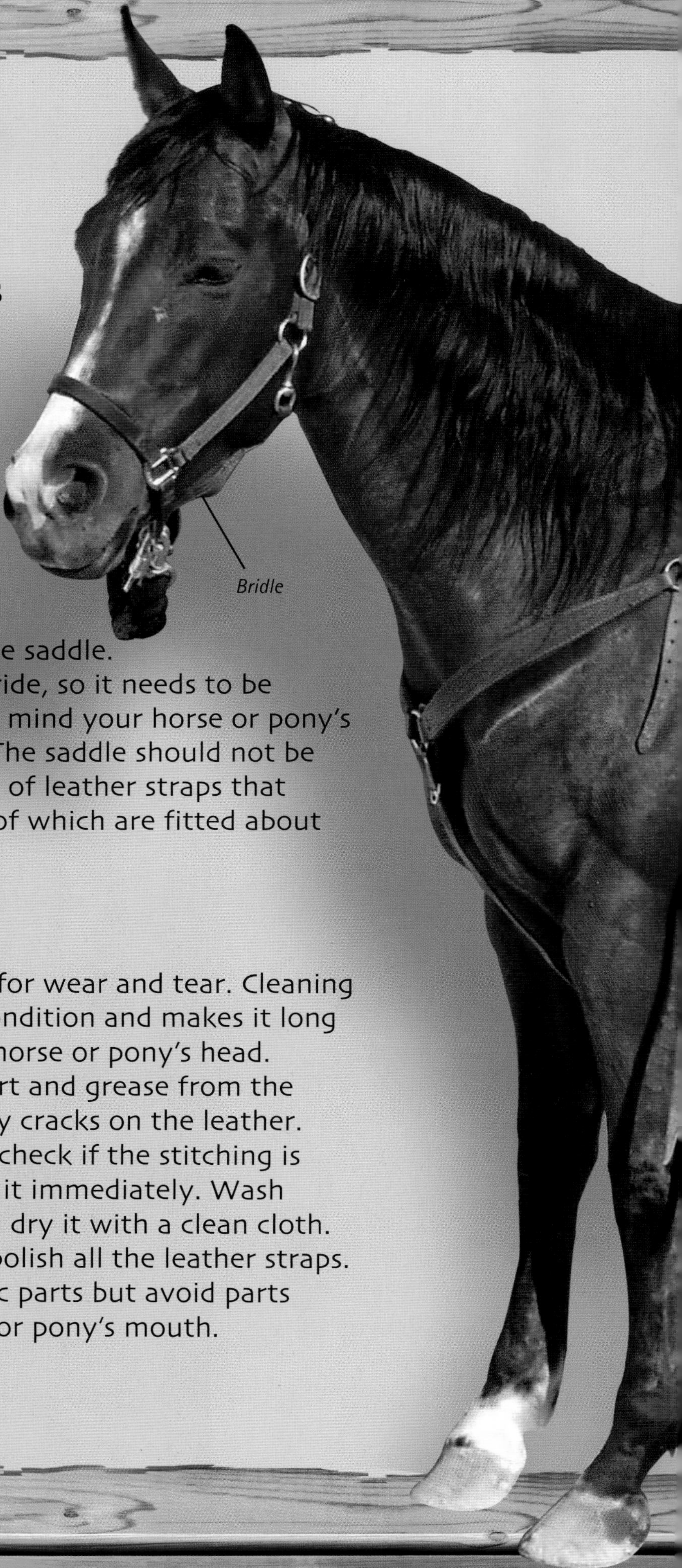

Bridle

Tack it Up

The tack consists of the bridle and the saddle.
You will sit on the saddle when you ride, so it needs to be comfortable. You should also keep in mind your horse or pony's comfort when you choose a saddle. The saddle should not be hard on their back. The bridle is a set of leather straps that includes a headstall, bit and rein, all of which are fitted about your horse or pony's head.

Cleaning the Bridle

Tack should be cleaned and checked for wear and tear. Cleaning the tack regularly keeps it in good condition and makes it long lasting. Remove the bridle from the horse or pony's head. Use a damp sponge to remove the dirt and grease from the leather straps. Check carefully for any cracks on the leather. Do not forget to check the seams to check if the stitching is sound. If any part needs mending do it immediately. Wash the bit separately in soapy water and dry it with a clean cloth. Now use saddle soap and a cloth to polish all the leather straps. Likewise, use metal polish on metallic parts but avoid parts that come in contact with the horse or pony's mouth.

Spotless Saddle

To clean the saddle you have to first strip it of stirrup and girth. Then place it on your lap and use a damp sponge to clean it. Check carefully for wear and tear. Then work on the stirrup leather, girth and girdle similarly. Shine the leather with saddle soap and metals with polish for a smart look. You may cover it with a cloth to keep it clean before the next ride. Always store the tack in a damp-free place.

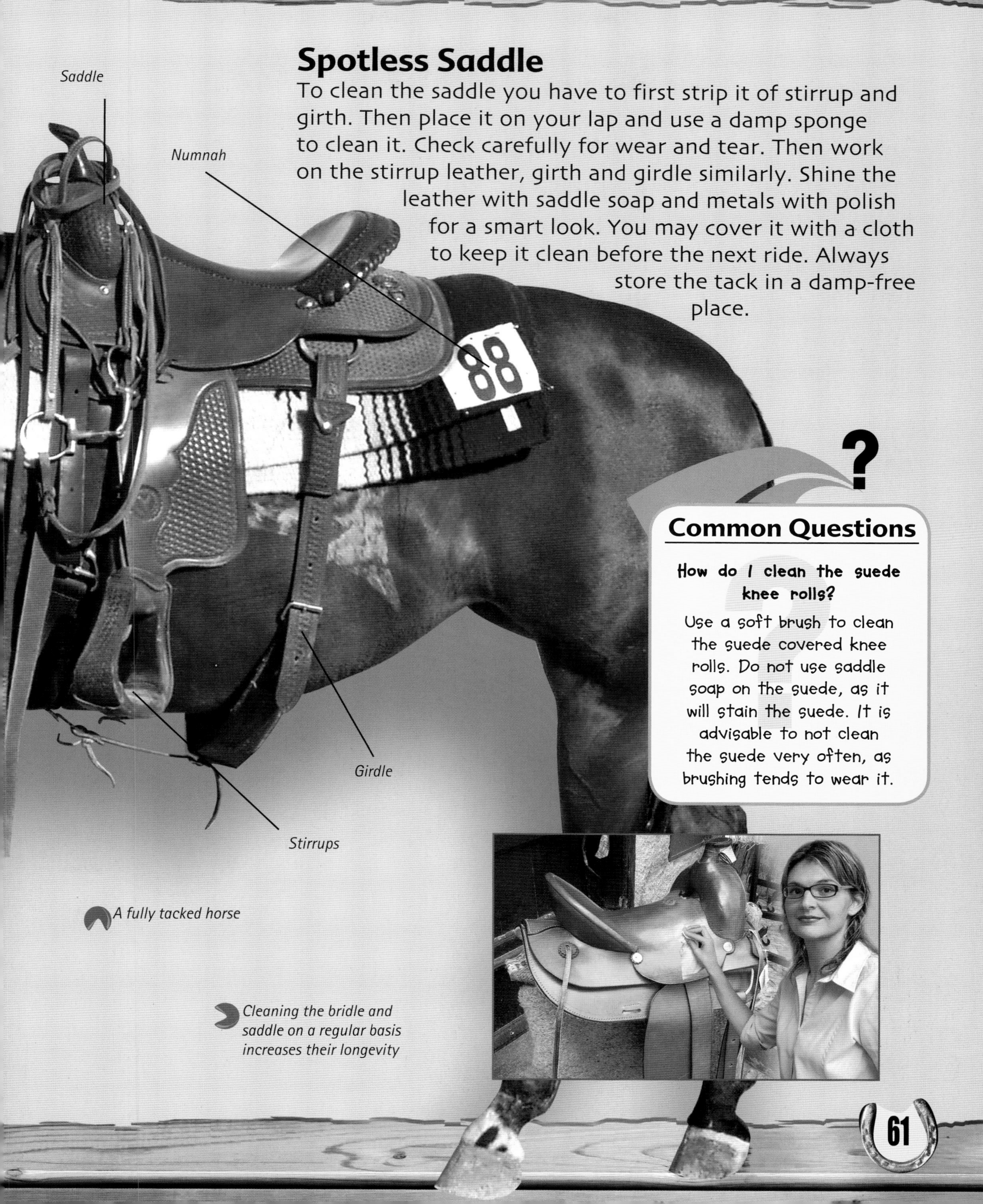

A fully tacked horse

Cleaning the bridle and saddle on a regular basis increases their longevity

Common Questions

How do I clean the suede knee rolls?

Use a soft brush to clean the suede covered knee rolls. Do not use saddle soap on the suede, as it will stain the suede. It is advisable to not clean the suede very often, as brushing tends to wear it.

Visiting the Vet

Just as you have a doctor who checks you regularly, your horse or pony needs veterinary attention too; you must fix a vet for their treatment and care. They should check the health of your horse or pony regularly and give it all the shots needed.

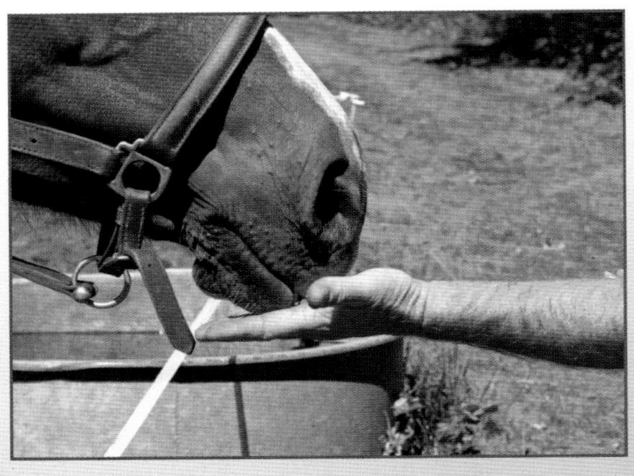

A man feeding de-wormer to a horse

A vet examining a horse with a stethoscope

Annual Shots

It is said that prevention is better than cure. Your horse or pony does not only need a vet when they are sick or have an injury. Since they are at risk to diseases all the time, they need some preventative medicines to keep good health. They need to be guarded against tetanus and equine influenza and require annual vaccinations for the prevention of these. Other annual vaccinations include anti- EEE WEE VEE and anti-rabies shots. The vet maintains a medical chart for your horse or pony so you know when a shot is due.

Regular Doses

Apart from annual shots a regular de-worming programme is a must as your horse or pony can pick up worms while grazing. If not treated these worms can be extremely harmful for them. De-worming is done every six weeks, but at certain times of the year it is done more often. Wormers usually come in powders that can be mixed into feed. You must ensure that your horse or pony eats them. Most horses and ponies do not make a fuss about their medicine. But if they do, try giving them the medicine with a cube of sugar.

Million-Dollar Smile

Dental care is as important for your horse or pony as other treatments. Infections in gums is not only painful but breeds several diseases too. You must check their teeth during grooming and call the vet incase of any dental problem. The teeth of your horse or pony need to be floated regularly: floating refers to the rasping and smoothing of teeth that develop sharp edges due to constant chewing. With the advancement in instruments, equine dentistry has improved greatly, to the benefit of your horse or pony.

A horse or pony's dental care is important for its overall health

Top Tips

Horses and ponies with dental problems will show some signs. Apart of external inflammation of gums, they will eat less and there will be more undigested food material in their dung. They might emit a foul odour from their mouth. There might even be swelling of the face. They will tend to toss their heads and chew the bit. It is important to identify dental problems early and treat them properly.

First Aid

You must have a first aid kit in your stable. You should also learn the basics of giving first aid before the vet arrives in cases of emergency and injury.

In Case of a Fall

One thing you must always remember is to not panic, even in the case of the worst emergency. It is important that you stay calm; only then will your horse or pony be calm. Do not move the horse or pony unless it is absolutely essential to do so. Remember, if they have got a fracture then moving around is not only painful but dangerous too. Call the vet. Make sure that you gather your horse or pony's vital signs before the vet arrives so as to give him the information. Reassure your horse or pony until the vet comes.

A first aid box or kit with all the essential products is a must for every stable

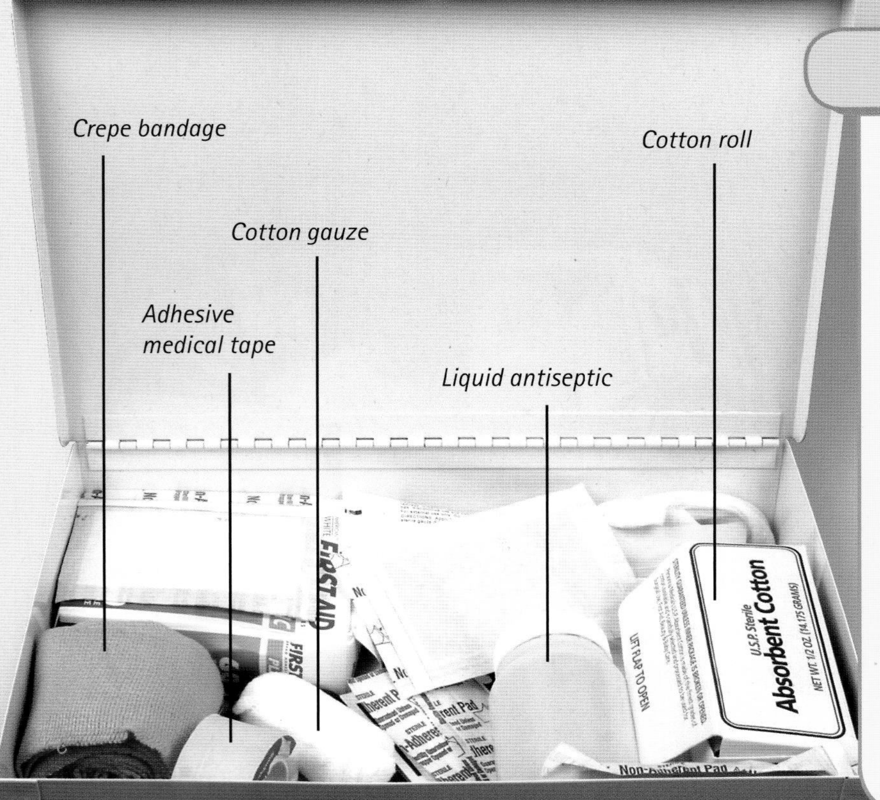

First Aid Kit

- *Large roll of cotton*
- *Rolls of cotton gauze*
- *Rolls of crepe bandage*
- *Adhesive medical tape*
- *Salt*
- *Wound powder*
- *Liquid antiseptic*
- *Antiseptic cream*
- *Veterinary thermometer*
- *Scissors*
- *Tweezers*
- *Clean bowl*
- *Torch*
- *A syringe of Tetanus Antitoxin and a Tetanus booster in the refrigerator*

Flesh Wounds

First of all, locate the wound and the nature of the injury. When you have identified it, act quickly. First clean the wound with clean water to remove dirt and debris. Then use saline water or antiseptic liquid to cleanse it thoroughly and prevent infection. Repeat till you are sure that the wound is clean. Use cotton to apply antiseptic cream in the area. If the wound is not too deep keep it open, otherwise dress it with gauze. If the wound is deep pad it with a sterile padding and if bleeding continues call the vet.

Top Tips

The basic first aid principles are to catch and calm the horse or pony, assess the extent of the injury, give proper first aid, gather their vital signs and then seek veterinary advice. Remember to replace tetanus syringes when the expiry date is over. Only attempt to give your horse or pony a shot if you are trained to do so.

All injuries to your horse or pony must be treated without any delay

A Guide to Taking Care
of a Cuddly Companion
Cats &
Kittens

Introduction

Are you a cat lover? Are you planning to bring home a new kitty? That's a lovely idea. But you need to know a lot of things before you actually go and buy a furry companion for yourself.

Oriental cats make very good pets because they bond well with humans

Other Family Members

Check if your parents are equally happy and glad about you bringing home a new cat or kitten. Not all people like pets at home. Also, some family members might prefer a different type of animal. Make sure you have the right kind of friendly atmosphere at home and that your cat or kitten will be treated lovingly as a pet and not a pest.

Things You Need to Know

You should know about the behaviour of cats and kittens: about different breeds and particularities; about health and general care; about what they like and what they don't. You should also register your cat or kitten with a vet. You should have some idea about the charges and other expenses involved in keeping a pet. Consult your elders and make sure you can afford all the expenses. You also need to find the right places to buy a new cat or kitten.

Consult Your Friends

Some of your friends might have pets at home. Share their experiences and take advice from them. Make notes of important points you learn from them, and check with an expert if all the information is true. You may also talk to other people you trust.

Cat Breeds

There are many breeds of cat in the world. Many of them are good natured, nice and adorable. The Cat Fancier's Association recognises 39 breeds.

Siamese Cats

Siamese cats originate from Thailand, and were previously known as Siam. Now they are found in many houses in England and other countries. They have beautiful blue eyes and are very loving in nature. Siamese cats are very friendly and can mix well both with children and adults. They are intelligent animals and should become friendly with other pets in the house. These cats also require little grooming. Siamese cats are a calm breed but are known for their unique voice.

Persian Cats

It is believed that Persian cats were orginally found in Persia (modern day Iran). Now these cats can be found all across the globe. With their large expressive eyes, rounded ears, high nose, and chubby cheeks they are loving and affectionate animals. They mix well with other pets in the family. Hence, Persian's are a popular breed. They have very soft and long hair. Persian cats have a strong build and easily adapt to their environment. However, they require a lot of grooming and care. There are many types of Persian cats. The famous Himalayan cat is a well-known Persian breed.

Siamese cats have almond shaped eyes and a flat coat

Oriental cats make very good pets because they bond well with humans

Top Tips

In very humid and warm weather conditions, you must brush your cat or kitten regularly. Shedding the excess fur will help them to feel light, comfortable and happy.

Persian cats need regular grooming to maintain their long and dense fur

Other Breeds

The Abyssinian breed is very graceful. With big expressive eyes and a shiny coat, they look very attractive. They can live for more than 20 years. Oriental breeds of cat are known for their striking green eyes and colourful bodies. Oriental cats have very long tails and soft, silky hair. They are very playful cats and love to make a lot of noise. They are usually very active and love to be with their master.

Buying a Cat

You can buy your cats or kitten from one of several places. Once you have made up your mind to buy a cat or kitten, you may visit a breeder, a rescue home or a pet shop.

Breeders

Cat breeders will carefully plan and breed species to produce nice, fit and healthy cats and kittens. They take note of the health and temperament. Cat breeders not only sell their breeds, but sometimes use their choicest cats and kittens for public shows. But not all breeders are equally reliable. It is always better to buy your cat or kitten from a reputed breeder. It's a good idea to find a breeding club to help you identify the right breeder.

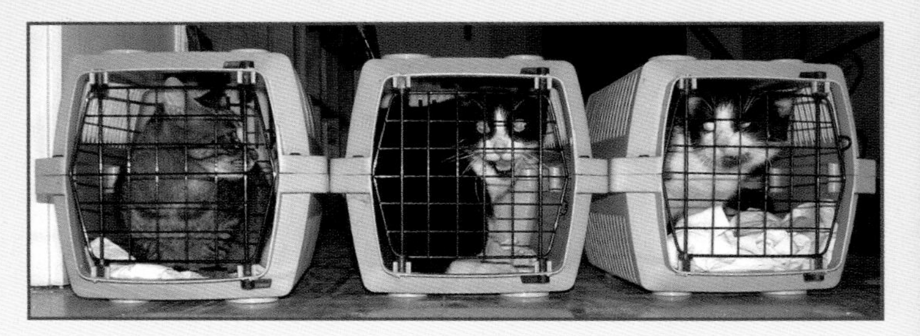

Visit several breeders before you choose the cat or kitten you want to buy

Rescue Home

Many cats and kittens each year are abandoned and left homeless. Rescue homes take care of such cats and kittens and look after the sick or abandoned. Only after the cats and kittens are healthy again and have learnt good manners are they sold. If you buy a cat or a kitten from a rescue home, you can be sure of its health and temperament. However, buying a cat and kitten from a rescue home may be a lengthy process. They will ask you to fill-in forms and will do a reference check to see if they are selling the cat or kitten to someone who can take good care of it.

Rescue homes are a good option because they take very good care of pets and will give you a nice and healthy cat or kitten

When you go to buy your cat or kitten from a pet shop, always ask about the breed and other details of the pet

Common Questions

How do I find out about cat or kitten breeders in my town?

You can locate a good breeder though pet clubs. You can also look for advertisements in newspapers to locate breeders in your town. Always take an adult with you before you finalise on buying your cat or kitten.

Pet Shops

Pet shops are another common place where you can get a cat or kitten. Cats and kittens in pet shops come either from private owners or from commercial cat and kitten farms. Unlike a reputed breeder, farms are usually less concerned about the health and temperament of the pets. Often there will also be less information about the background or breeding history of the cats and kittens available there.

Hello Kitty

When you bring a cat or kitten home for the first time they will need some time to adapt. But don't worry, they will gradually become familiar with the new environment, as well as the people and other pets.

This is Your Home

As the cat or kitten enters your home, take it around to make it familiar with every part of your house. Initially, your new pet might feel threatened. So, make sure you give your cat or kitten a space to hide when scared. It is best to confine it to a room for a few days. Spend a lot of time with your pet in that room.

You need to make your pet cat or kitten feel comfortable in its new surroundings

Other Pets

It is best to think carefully before buying a cat or kitten. Consider the nature of the other pets you have at home as well as the cat or kitten you plan to buy. A lot depends on compatibility when there is more than one pet in a house. Quiet and serious cats or kittens may find it difficult to be around more active animals. While your new cat or kitten is confined to one room, try to gradually make them aware of the other pets' presence. With time, they should happily mix freely.

Your new cat or kitten may fight with other pets in the house before it gets familiar with them

Top Tips

Always be around when you are letting your new cat or kitten and other pets to interact for the first time. Let this happen in an open space, so that if one of them attacks the other, the latter can easily escape.

Your new cat or kitten may take some time before it starts interacting with the other pets in the house

Watch How They React

If the new pet starts fighting with existing pets, take your new pet back to its room. Keep it there for a few days and try the whole thing over. If the other pet is a bigger or more powerful animal like a dog, be very careful, because chances are that the dog might attack your cat or kitten. If the cat or kitten is in danger of being attacked and cannot escape, it might even attack you out of fear.

Kitty Party

Cats and kittens are often fussy when it comes to food. They have strong likes and dislikes. To keep your cat or kitten healthy, you should know what they like to eat and what is good for their health.

Dry or Wet?

There are broadly two types of cat food available in the market — dry and wet. Dry food has very large amounts of carbohydrates. Too many carbohydrates can be harmful to your pet, so it needs a balance of both dry and wet food. Wet food in moderation is good for your cat or kitten. The proportion of protein in wet food is higher than that in dry food.

Common Questions

Can lack of water cause a cat or kitten to dehydrate?

Yes, reduced water intake causes dehydration, can cause kidney related diseases and, in the worse cases, death.

Your cat or kitten should be given food to balance proteins and carbohydrates

Meat versus Plants

Proteins found in dry cat food are mostly plant based. But your cat or kitten needs meat-based proteins to stay fit and healthy. This is found in wet food. When choosing your cat or kitten's wet food, make sure you choose a reliable provider. Check the label to be sure of the contents and pick wet food that shows a high meat content. Some wet food might come in jelly and some might come in gravy. Both contain healthy minerals and fats that your pet needs. They might, however, have a preference, so try both to see which they like more.

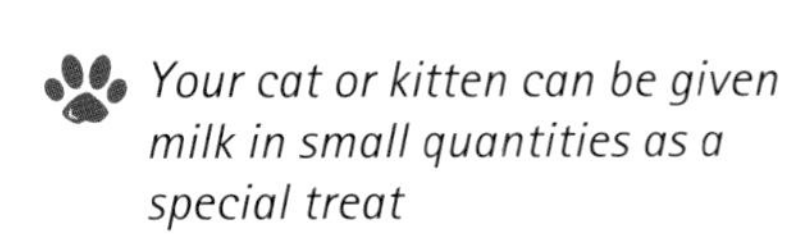

Your cat or kitten can be given milk in small quantities as a special treat

Water, Water

In the wild a cat or kitten's natural prey would contain about 75% water. You should ensure that your cat or kitten recieves this much water even when it eats cat food. Cats and kittens usually don't drink a lot of water as their food will provide most of what they need. However, it is still vital that you keep a fresh supply of clean water always available to your pet.

Cats and kittens love to catch mice

Regular combing of the fur coat of your cat or kitten will ensure that there are no lumps or mats of unwanted hair

Taking Care

You should regularly clean and groom your cat or kitten. This will help keep them hygienic, healthy and safe from diseases.

Combing

You should buy a special comb for your pet. Your cat or kitten's hair should be combed regularly. Choose a time when both you and your pet are in a relaxed mood. Your cat or kitten might become very restless when you start combing their hair. Begin by gently stroking, scratching and tickling the cat or kitten. You can start combing once you put it at ease. Your cat or kitten may have patches of matted hair. If you comb forcefully through such lumps of hair, you will hurt your pet, so be gentle.

Cleaning

Cats or kittens do not require bathing everyday. But sometimes they need to be given a wash. Wash your cat or kitten with lukewarm water. Never pour water directly on the head. Always use a cat shampoo while bathing your cat or kitten and be sure to wash out all the shampoo after cleaning it. Remove as much moisture as you can using a soft towel. Avoid using hair-dryers. Say nice things to your cat or kitten while cleaning. This will help your pet feel comfortable.

Nail Care

Your cat or kitten has what are known as retractable claws. These claws are very sharp and are always growing - much like your fingernails do. The cat or kitten uses these claws to help it grip when climbing and jumping. It will also use its claws when it hunts or, indeed, when it needs to defend itself. These sharp claws can be a nuisance in the home if your pet scratches your furniture. the best way to avoid this is to buy a scratching pole.

Top Tips

You should clean your cat or kitten's ears regularly. Ear mites often grow in their ears. This can be quite painful and even quite harmful for your pet unless cleaned properly.

Use cat shampoo to give your cat or kitten a clean and sparkling look

Your cat or kitten maintains their claws by scratching. Buy them a scratching pole to prevent them scratching your furniture

Protecting Your Cat

Your cat or kitten can lose weight and fall sick if it goes off its food

Like most animals, cats and kittens are prone to several diseases, some of which can even be fatal. You should be watchful if your cat or kitten contracts any of those diseases and take immediate action.

Fussy Eaters

Some cats can be fussy eaters. This is thought to be due to the fact that they are unable to taste sugars. Unlike most animals, cats are able to voluntarily starve themselves if they are presented with a food they are not used to, or if they become bored of a food they are fed regularly. Although it is rare for this self-starving to lead to injury, you should be aware of your pet's intake of food and watch for rapid weight loss. If in doubt, take your cat or kitten to the vet as soon as possible.

In case of a kidney disease, your cat or kitten should be fed food rich in Vitamin B

Kidney Diseases

You should take your cat or kitten for a BUN (blood, urine, nitrogen concentration) test every year after it is six years old. A BUN tests whether your cat or kitten has kidney related problems. Symptoms include scratching, fatigue, thirst, and frequent urination. In case of a kidney disease, your cat or kitten should be fed meat proteins, lots of water and food with reduced sodium.

Constipation

Constipation among cats and kittens is common. Sometimes constipation may lead to obstipation, which can be very dangerous. During constipation it becomes difficult for your cat or kitten to pass faeces. Obstipation is a state when your cat or kitten cannot pass faeces at all. This is a serious problem and needs to be checked by a vet. You should regularly monitor your cat or kitten's litter tray to make sure they are passing solid waste regularly.

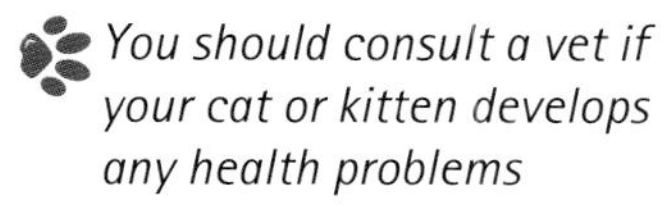
You should consult a vet if your cat or kitten develops any health problems

Common Questions

Should I add laxatives and cathartic drugs to my cat or kitten's food during constipation?

You may use laxatives, which are usually milder. But before adding cathartic drugs it is better you consult a vet. Cathartic drugs are very strong and can lead to diarrhoea.

Etikitty

Everyone wants well-behaved cats and kittens, who won't be a menace for the household. Cats and kittens, if not trained properly, can cause damage to furniture, carpets and even clothes.

Reward Them

While training your cat or kitten, don't try to force them or scold them if they do something wrong. Reward them when they do as you want. They should get the feeling that it is convenient and better to be well behaved rather than unruly. Cats or kittens are not expected to learn by mere instructions, but slowly acquire good habits by practice followed by rewards.

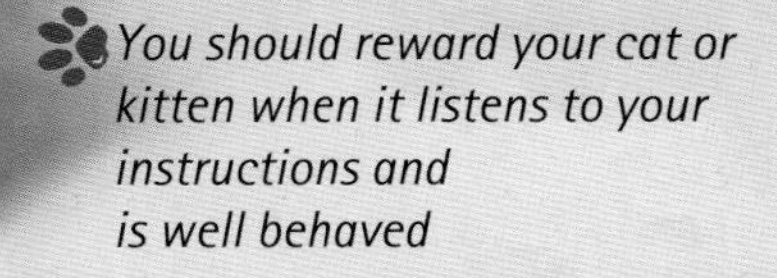

You should reward your cat or kitten when it listens to your instructions and is well behaved

You can buy different coloured litter boxes for your cat or kitten

Litter Training

Litter training is very important if you don't want your cat or kitten to spoil your home. You should follow a fixed routine when feeding your cat or kitten. This will ensure that your pet will relieve itself at more or less a fixed time. Stand near the litter box and call your pet from wherever it is. Do something to attract the cat or kitten towards the litter box (such as shaking a toy or some dry food). Make sure you have a layer of fresh cat litter in the tray because your cat or kitten's instinct is to scratch loose material over its faeces. Reward your pet when it uses the litter tray correctly.

Litter Tray Hygiene

Just as you keep the bathroom and toilet clean in your home, so you should keep your cat or kitten's litter tray clean. But, don't worry, you don't have to change the litter every day! You should remove faeces from the litter with a scoop every day or so. Once a week, throw away the litter and thoroughly clean the tray with soap and water. Allow the tray to dry before placing fresh litter back in the tray.

Top Tips

When cleaning out your cat or kitten's litter tray you might want to wear protective gloves. Remember your own hygiene when doing so: thoroughly wash your hands once you have finished and sterilise the area you have washed the litter tray out in.

Thoroughly clean out your cat or kitten's litter tray about once a week

You could buy a toy mouse for your cat or kitten to chase at home

Keeping Fit

Regular exercise keeps cats and kittens fit and healthy. Unlike a dog, which requires regular walks in order to stay fit, cats are very good at exercising themselves. However, you may need to buy a few toys to keep your cat or kitten active.

Cat in a Box

You can start with a ball or a crumpled piece of paper. Throw it on the floor and let your cat or kitten jump on it. You can also use a box and keep the ball inside it. Your cat or kitten will be curious to get in and see what is inside. Keep repeating this game to provide some fun both for you and your cat or kitten. You could even use a battery-operated mouse instead of a ball of paper. Your pet cat or kitten will have a lovely time trying to catch it.

Catch it if you Can

You could arrange something for your cat or kitten to chase around, thus building up its muscles as well as it being happily active. Your cat or kitten is predatory by nature and will love this chasing game. You can use balls, teaser wands or even mouse toys for this. You can also arrange something for the cat or kitten to climb, placing an object on top of it. There are many types of cat toys available in shops. Be creative and enjoy the moments you spend playing with your cat or kitten.

Love of Heights

Some cats and kittens will shown a love of high and sometimes dangerous places, such as the edges of rooftops. Cats have excellent balance and are also capable of falling significant distances without hurting themselves. However, especially with younger kittens, it might be wise to block-off more dangerous heights. Be warned though: cats are excellent climbers and, if they really want to get somewhere, they'll usually find a way!

You should keep an eye on your cat or kitten to try to prevent them from hurting themselves

Playing with balls of wool can be fun for your cat or kitten

Common Questions

**What is catnip?
Do all cats respond to it?**

Catnip is a herb. Most cats and kittens become hyperactive if exposed to catnip. However, kittens below three months do not respond to it. Most (but not all) grown up cats respond to catnip.

Beat the Heat

Your cat or kitten will need special care during summer, as heat and sun can be really dangerous.

Heat Stroke

Heat stroke is a potentially fatal condition, where the body organs cannot function due to exposure to heat. A cat or kitten's usual body temperature ranges from 100.5-102.5 Fahrenheit (38-39.1 Celsius). Make sure your cat or kitten has easy access to shade indoors during hot summer months. Cats and kittens are usually very good at keeping out of the heat themselves, but if you find your cat or kitten panting or dizzy, very weak, its gums turning dark red or very pale or bleeding from the nose, it could be signs of a severe heat stroke.

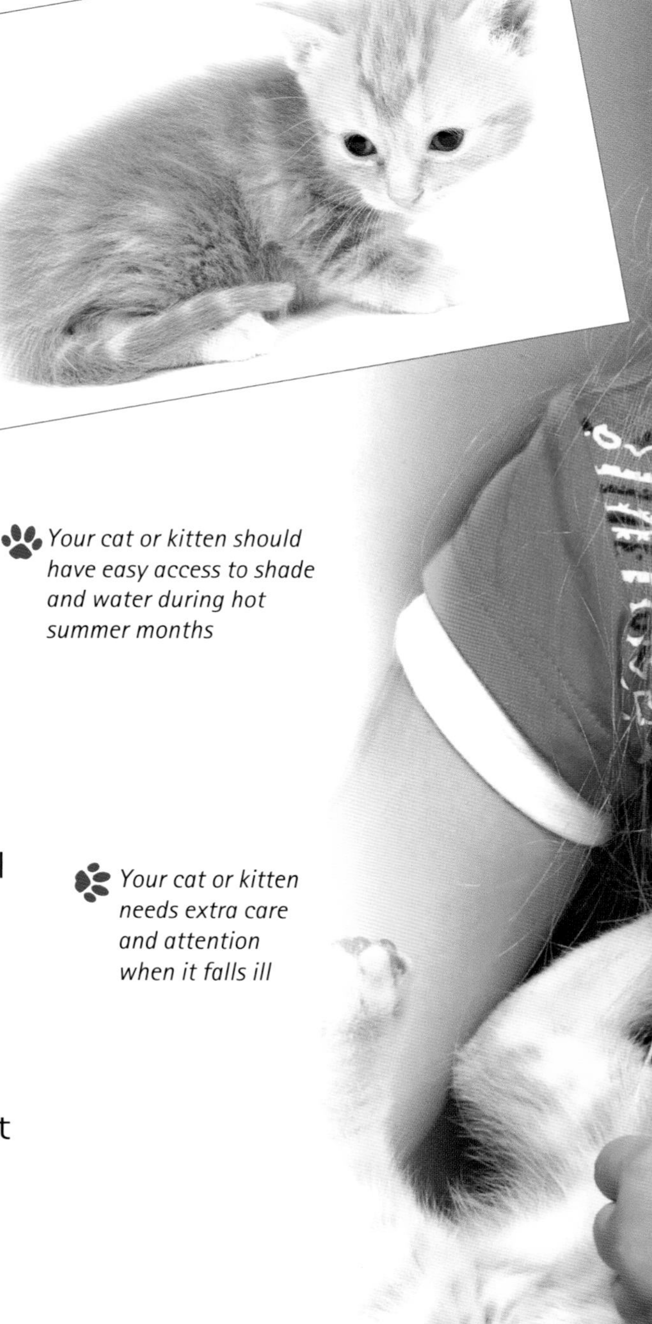

Your cat or kitten should have easy access to shade and water during hot summer months

Your cat or kitten needs extra care and attention when it falls ill

Dehydration

Heat stroke can lead to severe dehydration. Apart from sun stroke there could be several reasons for dehydration - like vomiting and diarrhoea, loss of appetite and reduced water intake, fever or blood loss. Ensure that your pet cat or kitten has easy access to a regularly-refreshed supply of water. Remember that your cat or kitten gets most of their liquid intake from food, so make sure they are fed properly too.

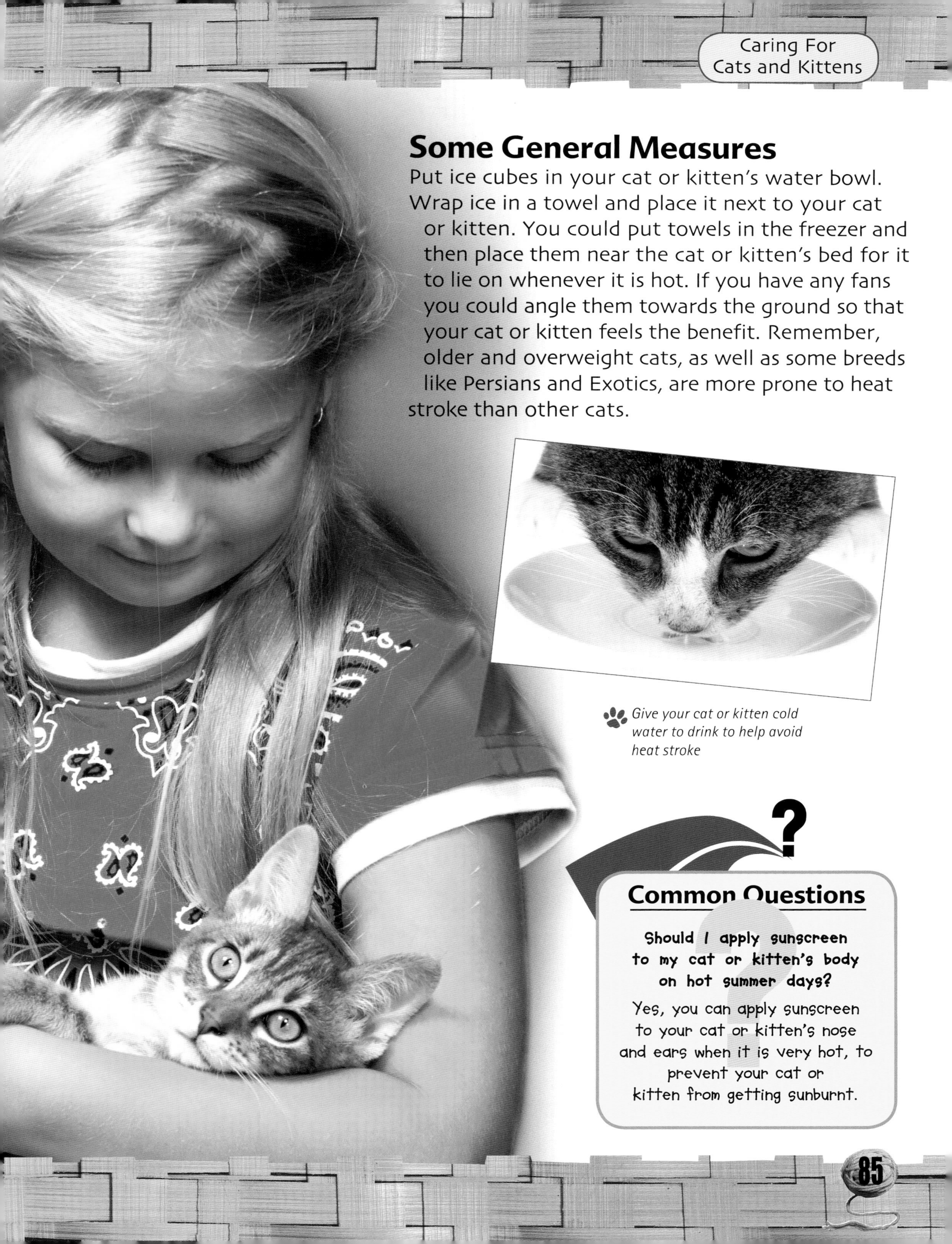

Some General Measures

Put ice cubes in your cat or kitten's water bowl. Wrap ice in a towel and place it next to your cat or kitten. You could put towels in the freezer and then place them near the cat or kitten's bed for it to lie on whenever it is hot. If you have any fans you could angle them towards the ground so that your cat or kitten feels the benefit. Remember, older and overweight cats, as well as some breeds like Persians and Exotics, are more prone to heat stroke than other cats.

Give your cat or kitten cold water to drink to help avoid heat stroke

Common Questions

Should I apply sunscreen to my cat or kitten's body on hot summer days?

Yes, you can apply sunscreen to your cat or kitten's nose and ears when it is very hot, to prevent your cat or kitten from getting sunburnt.

Wintry Nights

Like in summer, cats and kittens also need special care in winter. During winter months, cats and kittens should be kept warm. Providing a proper shelter for your cat or kitten is just the beginning of your responsibilities.

Keep it Warm

The room you have allotted to your cat or kitten to stay in should be insulated and properly heated. Your cat or kitten should not be left to sleep on the floor. Provide it with a thick and warm bed, as well as duvets and blankets to keep the cold away. Cats or kittens should also eat more in winter. This will add more calories, which in turn will help keep the body warm. If the temperature drops alarmingly during this season, do not let your cat or kitten outside. Keep it indoors so that it can be warm. If you do let your pet outside, make sure they have easy access in and out of the house so that they can come in easily when they are cold.

Let your cat or kitten play indoors during the winter months to keep warm and safe

Frostbite

If your cat or kitten spends too long outside when it is freezing, it may risk getting frostbite. You should be careful to remove any ice, snow or mud from your cat or kitten's feet as soon as it comes back. If it is frostbitten you will notice that your pet's skin has turned reddish, grey or white and the skin may also be scaly or peel off. Take your cat or kitten to the vet if you spot any of these symptoms.

Top Tips

Whenever you suspect frostbite, apply a warm and moist towel on the frostbitten areas before you call on your vet. This stops things becoming worse.

Frostbite will cause the skin of your cat or kitten to peel off and become extremely painful

You could dress up your cat or kitten during festive seasons

Holiday Food

Winter is a time when you love to party and eat lots of good food. This is the time for Halloween and Christmas. But it's important to remember that sweets, turkey, pork or any alcoholic drink are not good for your cat or kitten. Do not change their regular diet in winter, but you can increase the amount of food. Especially at Christmas, make sure that small bones, as well as small decorations (or anything else that could get caught in your cat or kittens throat), is kept out of reach.

Watch Out!

Be careful when your beloved little kitty roams about in your house. Many articles in your house could appear completely harmless to you, but may pose a real threat to your cat or kitten.

Be careful to never leave your pet cat or kitten unattended near anything hot or burning in the house

Fire and Electricity

Your cat or kitten can be easily attracted towards the bright flames of your fireplace. Burning candles, left unattended, may be dangerous too. Be careful when you have anything burning in the house. Wires and appliances should be kept out of your pet's reach. Never leave a hot iron unattended when your cat or kitten is around.

Chocolates are Dangerous!

Chocolates, sweets and alcohol can be very harmful for your pet cat or kitten. Medicines, antifreeze and insecticides or other poisons could also prove fatal to them. They should not have access to any of these. Cats and kittens might like the taste of chocolates but you must not let them have them. Chicken bones can lead to choking and should be kept away. Keep away other small objects that could be easily swallowed by your cat or kitten. There are also some types of plant that you shouldn't keep in the same house as a cat or kitten.

Chocolates and sweets can be extremely harmful for your pet cat or kitten

High baby cots will help keep your cat or kitten away from a baby at home

Common Questions

Can the medicines we take in times of sickness help our cats or kittens?

Never try medicines for humans on your cat or kitten. Always consult a vet when your pet is sick.

Keep Babies Away!

If you have a young child at home, you need to be very careful. Cats or kittens have a tendency to curl up to the bodies of babies as they find them warm and very comfortable. This is potentially very dangerous. Always keep your pet cat or kitten away from babies. A cat net, that protect babies from such mishaps, is strongly recommended.

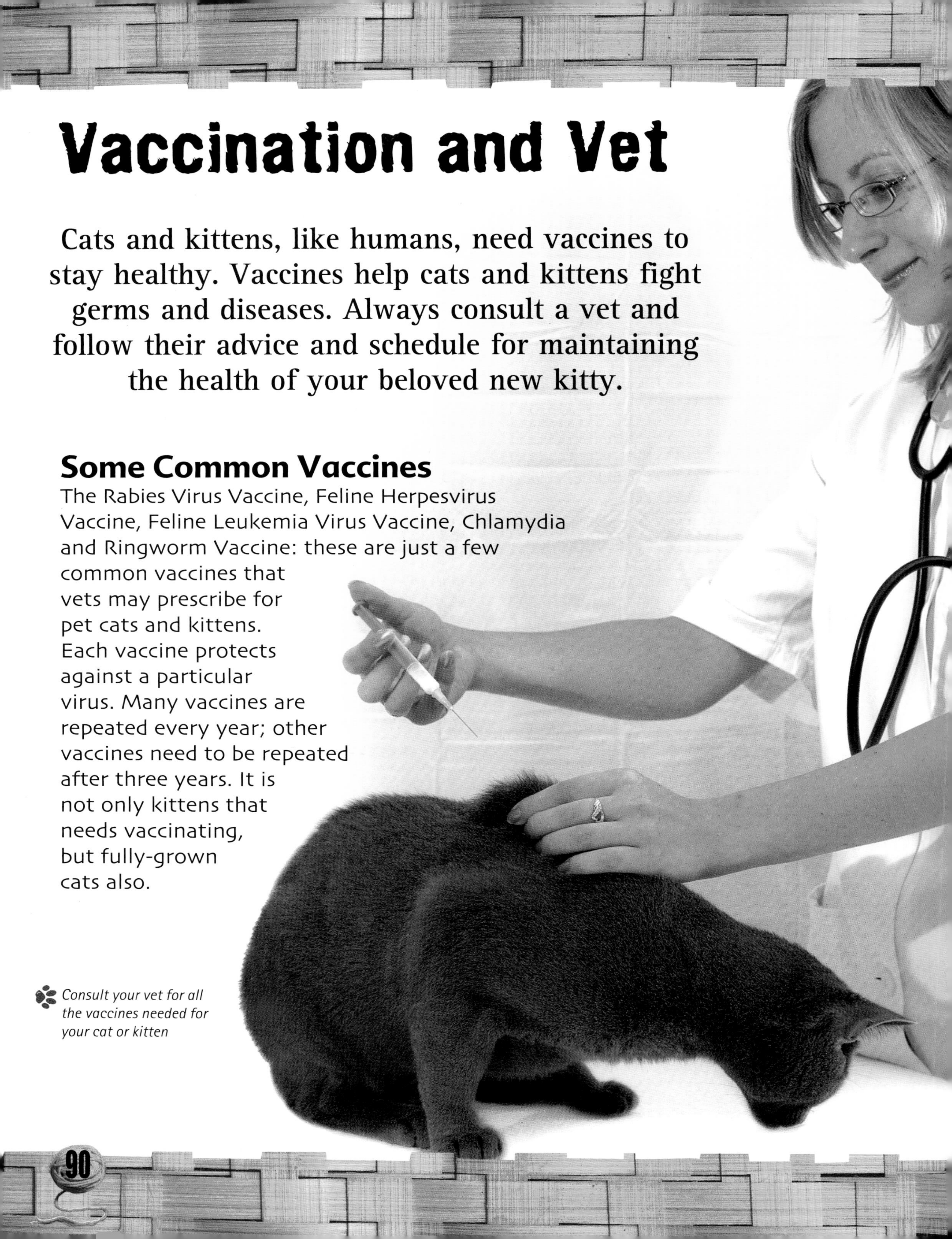

Vaccination and Vet

Cats and kittens, like humans, need vaccines to stay healthy. Vaccines help cats and kittens fight germs and diseases. Always consult a vet and follow their advice and schedule for maintaining the health of your beloved new kitty.

Some Common Vaccines

The Rabies Virus Vaccine, Feline Herpesvirus Vaccine, Feline Leukemia Virus Vaccine, Chlamydia and Ringworm Vaccine: these are just a few common vaccines that vets may prescribe for pet cats and kittens. Each vaccine protects against a particular virus. Many vaccines are repeated every year; other vaccines need to be repeated after three years. It is not only kittens that needs vaccinating, but fully-grown cats also.

Consult your vet for all the vaccines needed for your cat or kitten

Vaccination Side Effects

Vaccinating your cat or kitten can cause side effects. The reactions could be mild or very serious. In case of mild reactions your pet might catch a fever, sneeze and lose its appetite for a few days. There might be small swellings under the skin, which lasts for a few days. If any of these symptoms lasts for an unusually long time you should return to your vet for advice.

Top Tips

A vaccine for ringworm has just come out and is available in certain parts of the world. Check with your vet if the vaccine is available in your country. This may free your pet from worm related troubles.

Take your cat or kitten to the vet if you spot any unusual symptoms

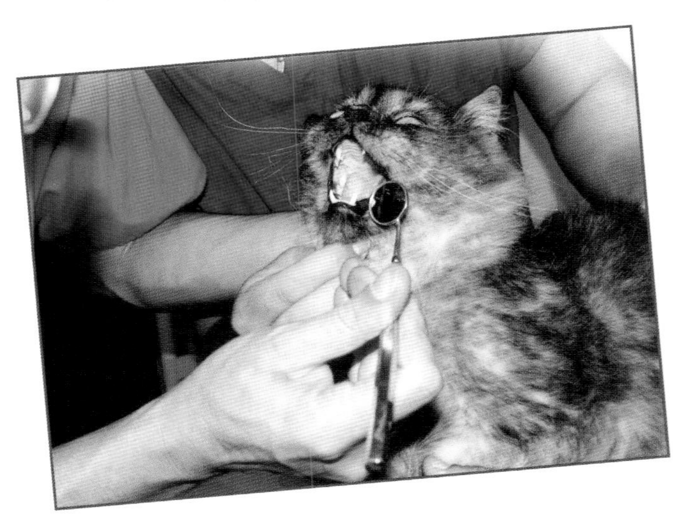

Your cat or kitten may eat grass when it does not feel well

Things May Get Serious

Serious allergies to vaccination are potentially fatal to your cat or kitten, but serious reactions are rare. In such cases, your cat or kitten may react immediately, or the reaction may occur after some time. Sometimes, tumours or lumps may develop on the area of the skin where the vet has administered the vaccine. Tumours may not surface right away, but may take several weeks or months to emerge. If you have any concerns you should consult with your vet. They will do everything possible to protect the health of your animal.

First-Aid

Your pets may have accidents and you should keep a first-aid box handy for your cat or kitten just in case.

You should follow an agreed schedule when taking your cat or kitten to the vet

Eye Drops and Ear Drops

Your first-aid kit should contain eye drops and ear drops. Ear drops should be used to clean your pet cat or kitten's ears regularly. You could also use olive oil or almond oil as ear drops for your pets. In case you have run out of eye drops and you need some urgently, you can make some saline solution yourself. Boil some water, then dissolve a little salt in it, before cooling it. This is a good remedy for times of emergency and can ease your pet cat or kitten's distress.

A vet checks the health of a cat's eyes

Antiseptic

You should always keep good antiseptic solution or cream. Some creams contain phenol and cresol which are harmful to cats and kittens, and should be avoided. You need to check the chemicals used in the antiseptic. Consult your vet about the right type of antiseptic for your kitty.

Always keep a tube of antiseptic at home for minor accidents

Other First-Aid Items

You should keep some fur-ball remedy, blunt-ended scissors, tweezers, and syringes. Syringes are not only needed to inject medicine, but also for liquid feeding. A thermometer, petroleum jelly and some plain kaolin mixture are also advised. Kaolin mixtures are used in the case of minor stomach problems. Do not forget to keep adhesive plasters, gauze, bandages and some cotton wool.

Common Questions

How do I restrain my cat or kitten when they are injured and in pain?

If your cat or kitten is in pain they may scratch or bite you if you try to apply first-aid.

Carefully hold them by the back of the neck and then press them down. You may also wrap them in a blanket to prevent them further injuring themselves by struggling.

Adhesive plaster

Antiseptic solution

Gauze

Crepe Bandage

Cotton Wool

Prepare a small first-aid kit and always keep it in a place where you can reach it easily

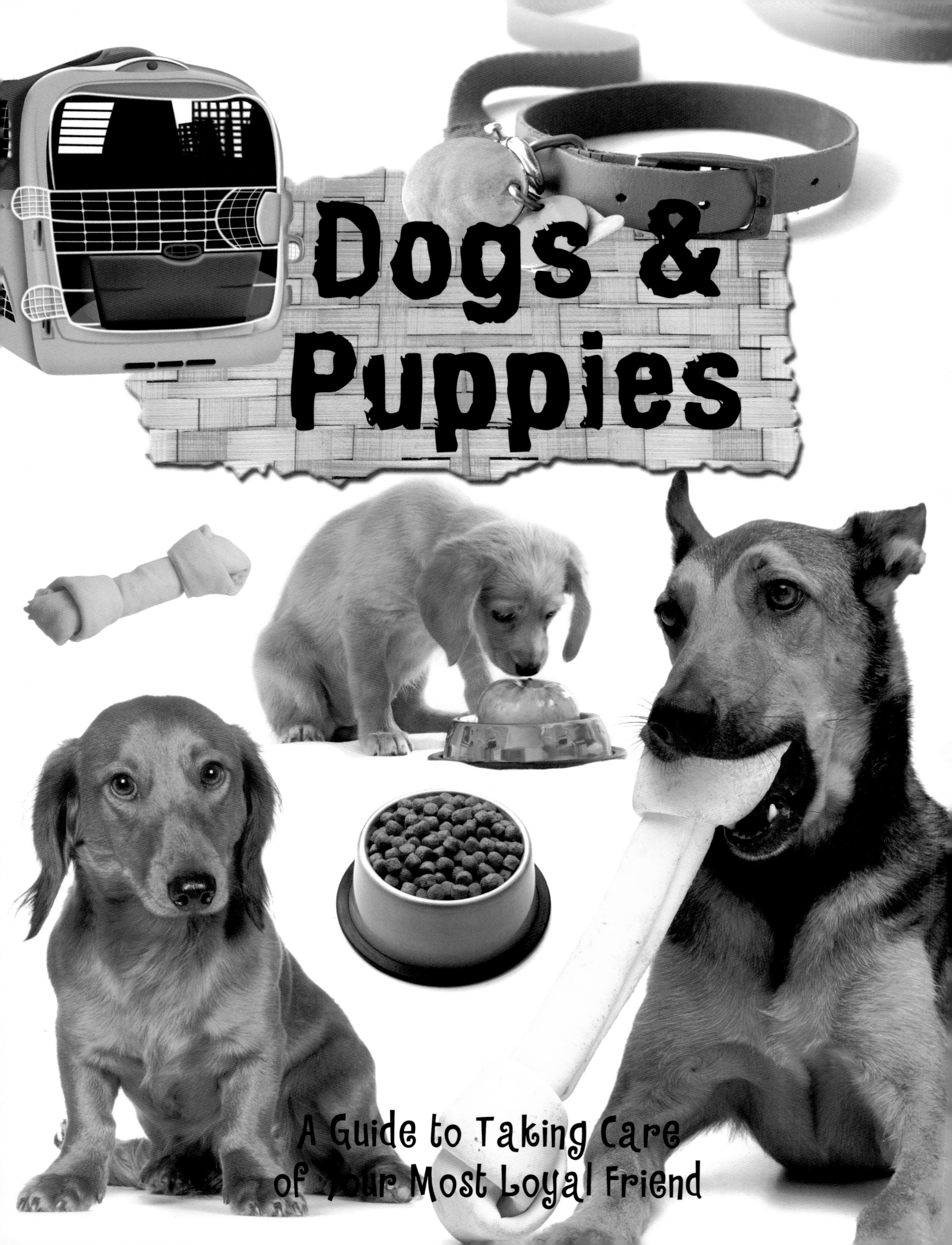
Dogs &
Puppies
A Guide to Taking Care
of Your Most Loyal Friend

Understanding Your Dog or Puppy

Buying a dog or puppy is a huge responsibility. You must ensure that your new pet is comfortable and healthy and you must care for it too.

A dog relies heavily on its sense of smell. Allow it to sniff you often so that it learns to recognise you

Top Tips

You should let your dog or puppy smell everything around the house when it arrives for the first time. This will introduce your dog or puppy to the house and make it feel at home.

Exercise is as important for your dog or puppy as it is for you

First Things First

At first, you and your surroundings will be new to your dog or puppy. It is important to communicate with it in a loving manner right from the beginning so that it can learn to trust you and form a bond with you.

Settling Down

Any dog or puppy will be restless in its new surroundings and it is your responsibility to make it feel wanted and cared for. Do not try to teach it to do tricks on the first day, nor force it to do things it does not want to do. Introduce it to your house and all the family members so that it feels like a part of your family.

o Show You Care

ringing a dog or puppy home is a big esponsibility. You have to look after your pet like ou would look after a baby. Your dog or puppy's ealth depends entirely on you. With the support f your family, you have to look after the diet f your pet. You also have to take the time o walk your dog or puppy regularly so that gets its exercise. You will need to teach manners so that it does not upset other amily members or dirty the house.

With a little love and affection your dog will become a part of your happy family!

One and Many

When buying a dog or puppy, it is important for you to know the different breeds available and the one that is most suitable to you and your family.

Breeds and All

There are two types of dogs — purebred and mixed breed. Each breed of dog has a distinct personality. Other factors that you must also keep in mind are the temperament, size of the dog, and its coat. Some breeds have traits, like hyperactivity or a tendency for barking, that may be a problem for you.

A dog is supposed to be a very loyal animal. Your dog can be your best friend

The fox terrier got its name as it was traditionally used to help hunt foxes

Little Fox

The fox terrier refers to two different breeds of dog: the smooth fox terrier and the wire fox terrier. The two terrier breeds are distinguished by their coats. The smooth fox terrier has a smooth, flat and dense coat, while the wire fox terrier has a coat with a dense, wiry texture. Both these breeds of terrier are quite friendly and enjoy being a part of the family and so make good pets.

Gentle Giants

The St. Bernard dog is a large breed of dog. There are two varieties of the breed — the smooth-coat and the rough-coat variety. The St. Bernard is an excellent choice as a family dog. They also make good watchdogs. Their sheer size can scare strangers! However, they are actually quite gentle. St. Bernards grow and gain weight very quickly. They can be prone to weak bones if they do not get proper food and exercise.

The St. Bernard is the heaviest breed of dog in the world!

Because of their good looks poodles are frequently seen in dog shows

Common Questions

Which is the most famous St. Bernard?

Barry, the brave St. Bernard, saved many lives. There is a monument to Barry in the Cimetière des Chiens, and his body is preserved in the Natural History Museum in Berne.

Dainty Poodle

Poodles comes in three sizes — standard, miniature and toy. The hair on the animal's body is curly and forms small clumps of curly ringlets. Poodles are intelligent, alert, and active. They are excellent watchdogs and are good pets. Poodles are also very easy to train.

The One I Want

After you have chosen the breed of dog or puppy you want to buy, there are some other things that you have to keep in mind before making the final decision.

How Do I Buy?

Try to buy your dog or puppy directly from a breeder. They will be able to tell you about the nature of each dog or puppy under their care. See for yourself how the puppy or the dog reacts when you try to pet it. If it is friendly at first, it is more likely to stay friendly when you take it home. You also have to decide whether you want a male or a female dog.

Buy a female dog only if you are sure that you will be able to take care of it if it has pups

Common Questions

Where else could I buy my dog or puppy from?

You could buy your dog or puppy from a rescue organisation. These organisations find homes for dogs and puppies that have been abandoned and have no home. These organisations also rescue dogs and puppies when they are not being treated properly.

Dogs in animal shelters and rescue organisations wait eagerly for a good home. You could take one as your pet and care for it

Going To a Pet Shop

You can buy your dog or puppy from a pet shop. While this is common, you should consider some things carefully before you do. A pet shop is unlikely to have as much knowledge of a particular dog or puppy that a breeder would have. Ask about the background of the dog or puppy and what its vet history is in terms of vaccinations.

Animal Shelters

An animal shelter is a good option if you want to give an orphaned dog or puppy a new home. Many dogs and puppies there will have been with a family before, so they might already be housetrained. Be aware though: sadly, some will have been mistreated in the past. You will have to love them to earn their confidence and love.

Giving It a Home

It is usually easier for puppies to adapt to new surroundings than dogs. But remember, puppies need more attention than dogs

Once you buy your dog or puppy, the next big step is to take it home with you and teach it to adjust to its new surroundings.

Comfort

Removing your dog or puppy from its familiar surroundings and making it settle down in your home can be quite a challenge. Get a new dog basket which it can call its own. It is also a good idea to initially use a blanket or a towel that it used in its previous home, as this will give it a sense of security. For the first few days or weeks, try not to leave your dog or puppy completely alone at home for too long. Being alone may scare it and make it irritable.

A Place to Stay

Just as you have your own room, your dog or puppy should have its own too! Find a warm and quiet place for the dog basket and then try not to move it too much so that your pet becomes comfortable. It is best to not allow your dog or puppy to sleep on the floor, sofa, couch or your bed as this encourages bad habits. Line your dog basket with a blanket to make it cozy and comfortable. When your dog or puppy is sleeping try not to disturb it.

Top Tips

Select a place for your dog or puppy's food and water bowls that is easily accessible to them, but out of the way of human feet. Once selected, keep the bowls in the same place. This way your dog or puppy will learn good food habits and won't be confused.

A Home of its Own

Your dog or puppy will want to make its basket its own space, so don't let any other pets go in the basket. The dog basket should be kept in the room where everyone in the family spends a lot of time. This will help it feel loved and a part of the family.

In some countries, larger dogs are kept outdoors in kennels

Puppies tend to be messy eaters, so you should pay special attention to their training

Making Friends

Once you've brought your dog or puppy home, you need to make it your companion and best friend.

You must make your dog or puppy feel comfortable in your home. This will help it become a faithful companion

A New Friend

To make sure that having a new dog or puppy at home is a happy experience, you should pay attention to the new pet's care and training closely. If you are friendly with your dog or puppy it will respond in a simlar way. Training your dog or puppy to listen to you or learn tricks can take some time. You have to be patient and keep trying until it learns.

Strict Rules

Make sure you do not get hurt when you play with your pet. Always use a toy during play, and throw the toy around so that your dog or puppy can run and fetch it. You must not play rough games with your dog or puppy because it might be cruel and your pet may be encouraged to bite. Buy toys your pet can chew on to discourage it from chewing things in the house that it shouldn't!

Dogs and puppies enjoy chewing bones as these make their teeth stronger

Things around the House

There are various things you can keep in the house to make your dog or puppy feel comfortable.

Water bowl

Dog collar

Food bowl

Chewy dog bone

Dry dog food

Dog cage

Common Questions

What should I do if my dog or puppy gets lost?

Do not panic if you cannot find your dog or puppy. Pets often run out of the house but come back soon. However, if your pet is missing for more than a day, you could put an advertisement in the papers with a photograph of your pet. You could also contact animal shelters and rescue groups in your area.

Feeding Habits

The health of your dog or puppy depends on you. You should give it a proper and balanced diet to keep it healthy and strong.

Ground Rules

Your dog or puppy should be fed twice a day. You should have fixed hours to feed your pet. Serve the food in a clean dish and put the dish in a place where your pet will not be distracted by something else while eating. If you have more than one pet, then feed each of them separately. This way you will know how much food each pet needs. This will also prevent one pet from eating up the food of another.

Your dog or puppy should have a clean bowl of its own to eat from

You should never over-feed your dog or puppy as this might lead to obesity and other health problems

Balanced Diet

Just like your diet, your pet's diet should have a proper balance of carbohydrates, fats, proteins, vitamins and minerals. Packaged dog food usually contains a proper mix. But remember that the appetite of dogs or puppies varies from breed to breed. Your pet should have clean drinking water throughout the day. But do not allow your dog or puppy to drink water just before a meal as this will spoil its appetite.

Dog biscuits are available in various shapes and tastes and make good treats for your pet dog or puppy

You must make sure that the dog food you feed your dog or puppy has all the ingredients necessary for its growth

Top Tips

Ask the vet if your pet needs any special vitamin or mineral supplement.

Some dog breeds need supplements to maintain a healthy coat and skin and good bone growth.

Delicious Food

Meat is an important part of the diet for dogs and puppies. You can buy meat in tins for your dog or puppy, but alternate this wet food with dry food for a balanced diet. You can also give your dog or puppy the odd scrap of leftover cooked meat as a treat, but don't give them too much as they are not designed to eat cooked meat.

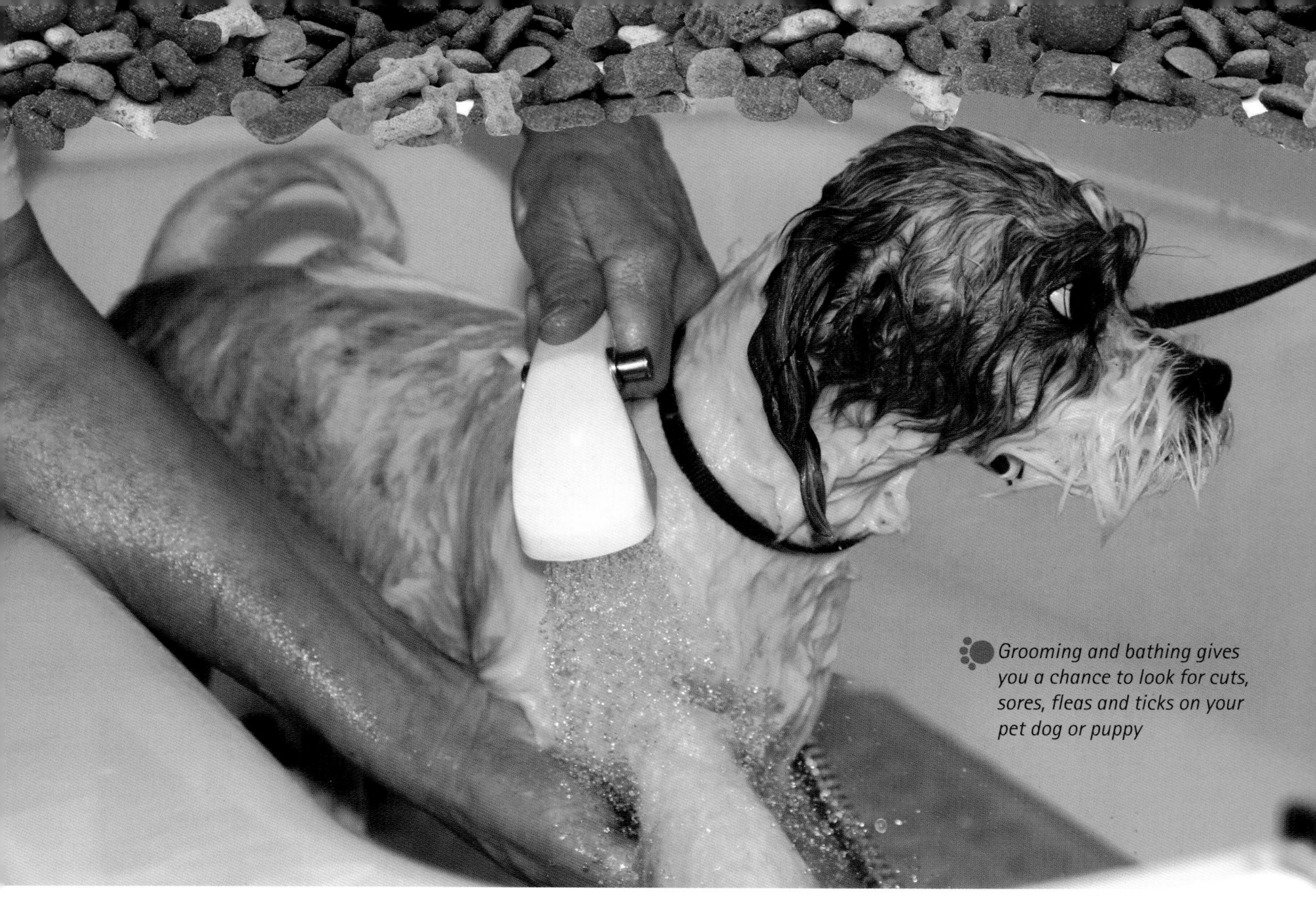

Grooming and bathing gives you a chance to look for cuts, sores, fleas and ticks on your pet dog or puppy

Grooming and Cleaning

Once you have a dog or puppy at home, it is essential to keep it clean and well groomed.

Groomed and Dressed

All dogs and puppies need to be groomed, but the frequency varies between breeds. Some dogs and puppies may need more frequent grooming than others. The most essential part of grooming is brushing and combing the hair of your pet, which helps to keep their coat shiny and skin healthy and free from ticks. A dog or puppy that has a long-haired coat should be brushed more frequently than one with short hair.

Washed and Cleaned

Dogs and puppies do not need to be bathed frequently. In fact, frequent bathing makes the skin of your pet dry as the natural oils present in the skin are lost. This can lead to infection and itching. While giving your pet a bath, use a good shampoo and conditioner designed for the coat of your pet. Make sure that you gently wipe your pet with a soft towel after you give it a bath.

Dog cologne

Grooming Tools

Here are some basic grooming tools for your pet:

- Fine Tooth Comb
- Grooming Brush
- Shedding Blades
- Small Scissors
- Tweezers
- Soft Wipes
- Dog Cologne
- Dog Mat
- Nail Clipper

Dog hair-brush

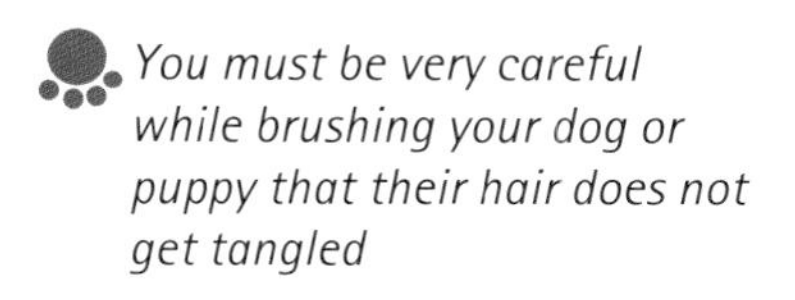

You must be very careful while brushing your dog or puppy that their hair does not get tangled

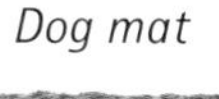

Dog mat

Fine-toothed comb

Common Questions

Do I need to find a professional groomer for my pet?

You may need a professional groomer if you do not have the time to clean and groom your pet. There are some breeds, like the poodle, that should have their coats styled in a particular way. It may be a good idea to take these dogs or puppies to a professional groomer once every couple of months.

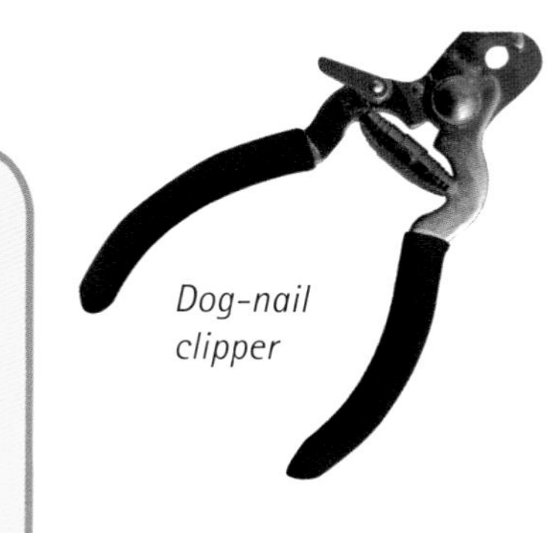

Dog-nail clipper

Ticking Away

You must always ensure that your pet is free of ticks and fleas. They are not only harmful for your pet, but for you as well.

A flea may be a tiny insect but it can be very dangerous. It will suck your pet's blood, which causes sores. Left untreated these sores may cause infection

Flea Attack

Fleas are the most common pests of dogs and puppies. If you find your pet scratching itself continuously, or if it has developed a skin rash, it has probably been attacked by fleas. When fleas bite a dog or puppy, it may develop red bumps on its tail and on the sides of its hind legs. You can use anti-flea shampoos and soaps for mild infections. But if it is a serious attack, you have to take your pet to the vet for proper medication.

Top Tips

Always make sure that you use a fine-toothed comb to clean fleas off your dog or puppy. The fleas get caught between the fine teeth easily. After that, drop the comb into a bowl of soapy water. This will kill the fleas at once.

A dog or puppy can pick up fleas from other dogs when taken out for walks, so it is a good idea to groom it afterwards

Ticking Pests

After fleas, ticks are the most common pests picked up by dogs and puppies. Look for them especially in the ears, and on the head, armpits and thighs. Not only are ticks harmful by themselves, they will also lead to other infections if they are not removed. You can use tweezers to remove ticks, but be very careful if a tick is embedded in the skin. Always wear gloves while removing ticks.

When you remove a tick make sure that you dispose it of well

Bugs and Bites

There are other bugs that bother dogs and puppies. Flies are a major nuisance for your pet. Some flies can bite the ears and neck of your dog or puppy and leave red marks. Apply an antiseptic cream to the infected area if you find these marks. Also ensure that your pet does not go out during the hottest part of the day. Dogs and puppies can also come into contact with other insects, like wasps.

Training Tactics

You must teach your pet some basic manners and to be well behaved so that it is a pleasure to have at home.

The Initial Scare

When you first bring your dog or puppy home, it may be very submissive and scared. Your pet still won't recognise you well and may feel threatened by you or some other member of the family. Over a period of time, it will get over this initial scare and develop its own signals to indicate what it wants. It will also develop a relationship with every person in the home.

The more time you spend with your dog or puppy, the more it will learn to trust and love you

Higher Education

After your pet has got over the initial scare, you can teach it to follow basic instructions, like when and where to sit or eat. This teaching process may seem difficult, but it should be practised by everyone at home. It is important to reward your pet when it has followed an instruction successfully. Getting a reward in the form of a biscuit or other treat will make it feel important and happy.

You need to be gentle with your dog or puppy while teaching it new tricks

By taking your dog or puppy for family outings you will make it feel welcome and a part of your family

Common Questions

What should I do if my dog or puppy bites me?

Initially your dog or puppy will not know whether it should bite or not. Do not allow it to place its mouth on your hand. If your pet does bite you, just walk away from it. Let it realise that it has just lost its playmate. Only return to your pet when it has calmed down.

Gentle Love

It is very important for you to be gentle with your pet. You can accompany an elder when your dog or puppy is being taken out for a walk or a visit to the vet. Never harm the animal by pulling its tail or dragging it by its collar or legs. Never hit your pet, no matter how angry you are.

Keeping Fit

It is important for your dog or puppy to get enough exercise and play so that it does not become sluggish or lazy.

Give your dog or puppy enough exercise so that it does not become obese or face other health problems

Fat or Fit

Obesity in your dog or puppy is quite a seroius problem if not checked immediately. Dogs or puppies that are fat face high risks during any kind of surgery and are more prone to injury. Many tend to lose the sheen on their coats and develop dry skin. You could prevent it by making your pet excercise. You could also give diet food to your pet, but consult your vet first.

Your dog or puppy initially might be scared of water but will follow you if you teach it to swim

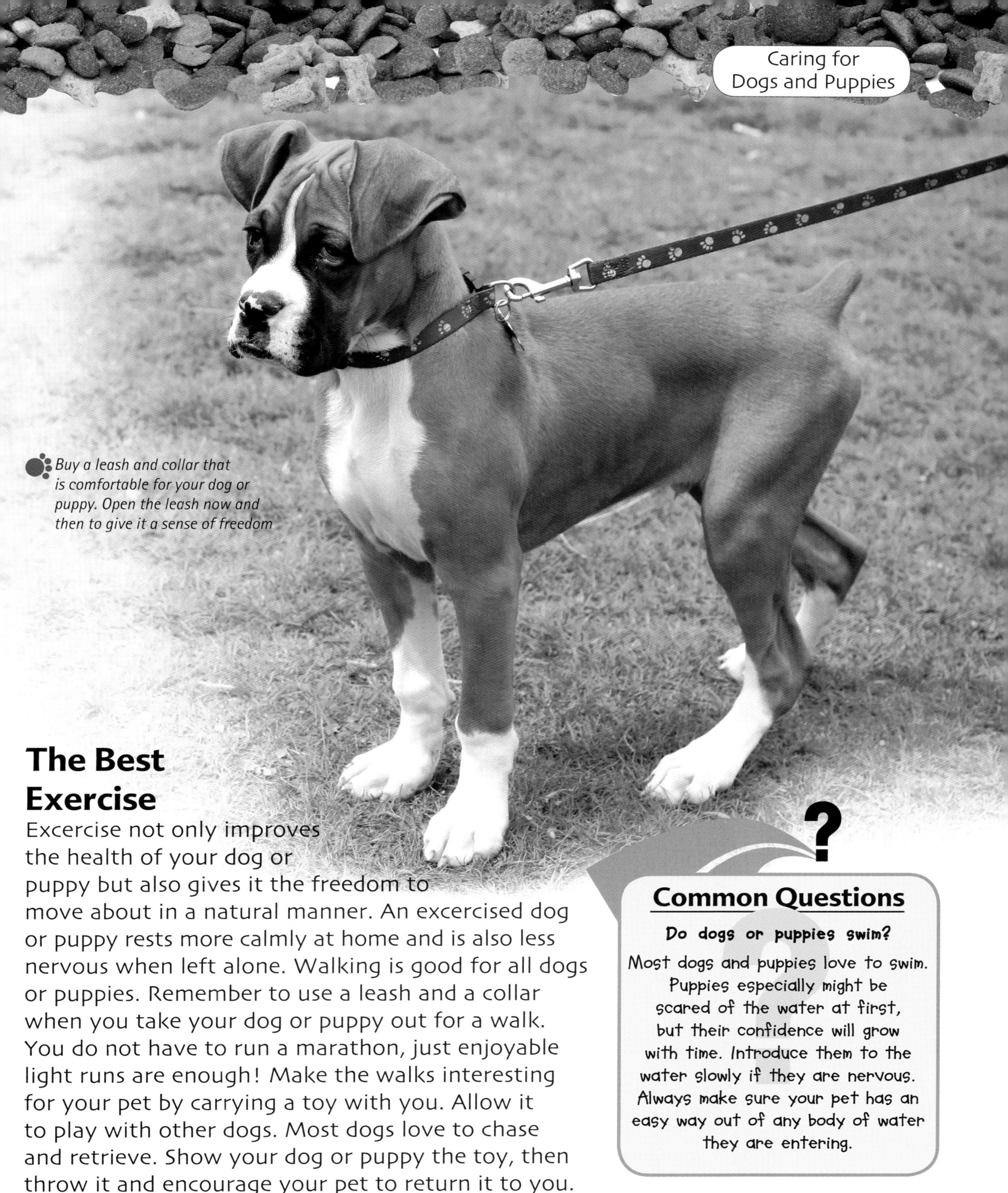

Buy a leash and collar that is comfortable for your dog or puppy. Open the leash now and then to give it a sense of freedom

The Best Exercise

Excercise not only improves the health of your dog or puppy but also gives it the freedom to move about in a natural manner. An excercised dog or puppy rests more calmly at home and is also less nervous when left alone. Walking is good for all dogs or puppies. Remember to use a leash and a collar when you take your dog or puppy out for a walk. You do not have to run a marathon, just enjoyable light runs are enough! Make the walks interesting for your pet by carrying a toy with you. Allow it to play with other dogs. Most dogs love to chase and retrieve. Show your dog or puppy the toy, then throw it and encourage your pet to return it to you.

Common Questions

Do dogs or puppies swim?

Most dogs and puppies love to swim. Puppies especially might be scared of the water at first, but their confidence will grow with time. Introduce them to the water slowly if they are nervous. Always make sure your pet has an easy way out of any body of water they are entering.

Happy Family

Your dog or puppy should fit into your home and be comfortable with all members of the family and any other pet that you may have.

Never leave your dog or puppy alone with babies and young children

Taking Care

Most dogs and puppies react in a very friendly and protective way when they see a new baby in the house. But you have to take some precautions to keep both the baby and the pet safe. Train it to be calm around the new baby. Do not allow your pet to play around the baby's cot. Your pet should be kept out of the baby's room. When a new baby joins the family it is more important than ever that the dog or puppy is kept in good health. Make sure they you de-flea them regularly and keep them up to date at the vets.

Living Together

Your dog or puppy can live peacefully with another pet in the house if trained to do so. In the beginning you must watch and supervise them when they are together. Remember that both dogs and cats are predators by nature and might not naturally get along. Slowly introduce your dog or puppy to your other pets and they should get used to each other.

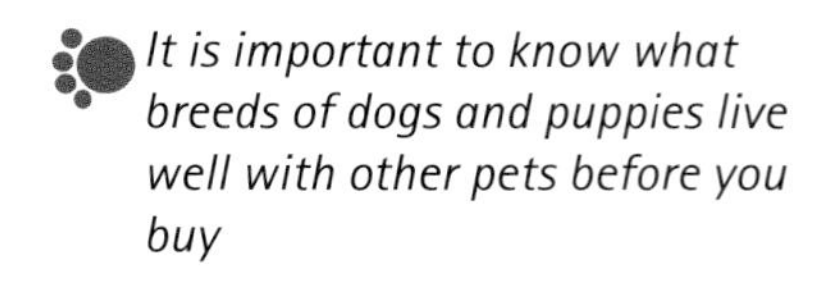

It is important to know what breeds of dogs and puppies live well with other pets before you buy

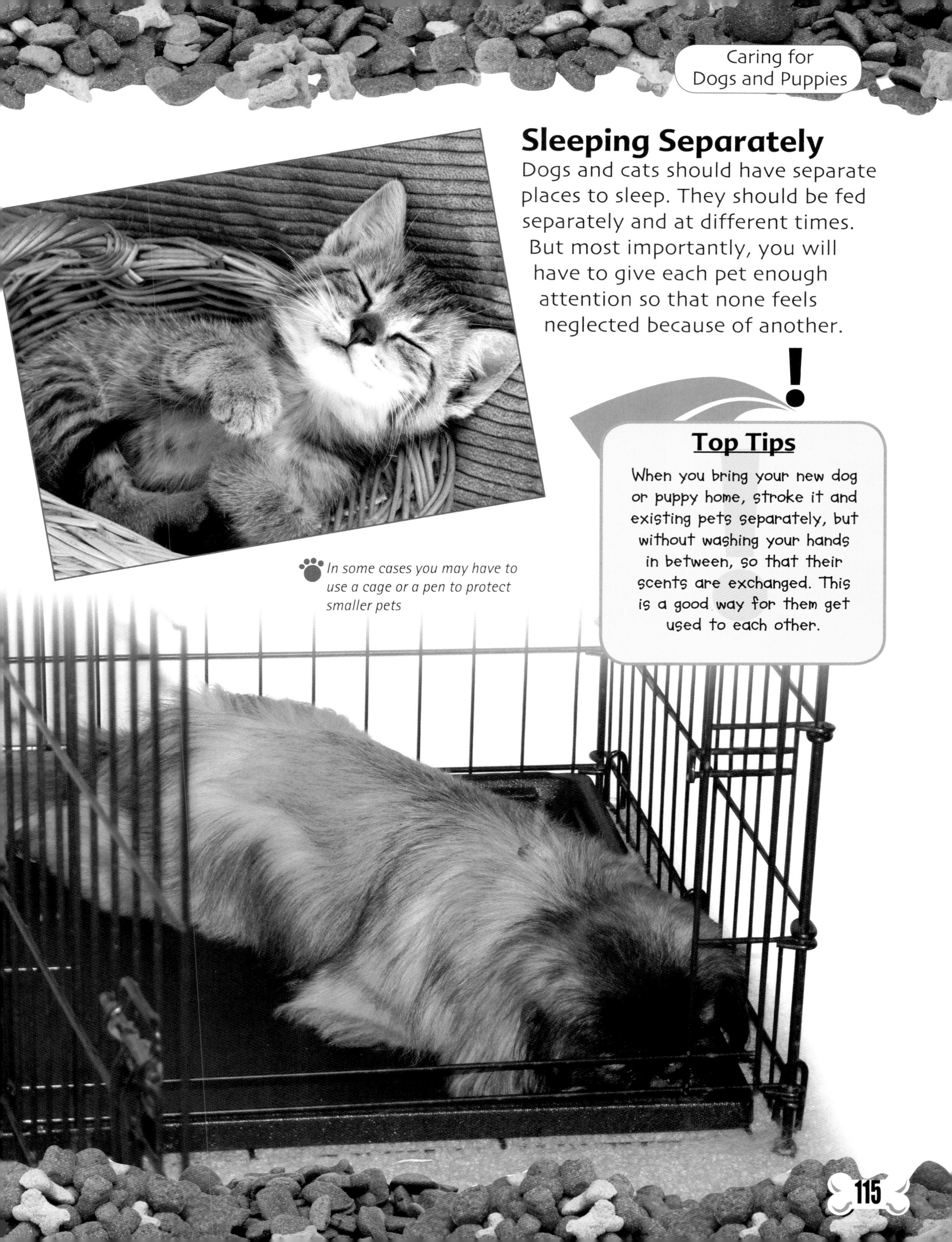

Sleeping Separately

Dogs and cats should have separate places to sleep. They should be fed separately and at different times. But most importantly, you will have to give each pet enough attention so that none feels neglected because of another.

In some cases you may have to use a cage or a pen to protect smaller pets

Top Tips

When you bring your new dog or puppy home, stroke it and existing pets separately, but without washing your hands in between, so that their scents are exchanged. This is a good way for them get used to each other.

Made For Each Other

A dog is a very loyal animal. Your dog or puppy can help you and your family in various ways.

A Friend in Need

Most breeds of dogs can be trained to become assistance dogs, also called guide dogs. They help and protect people with disabilities. They can help someone who cannot see to cross busy streets, use public transport and even find the way back home. Dogs can also be trained to recognise the sound of doorbells, phones, alarms or even the cry of a baby. Then they alert the person who cannot hear. But dogs need professional training to become assistance dogs, search dogs or police dogs.

Searching High and Low

Search dogs are used by the police to sniff for dangerous materials and by the fire service to find people trapped inside collapsed buildings or mines, or buried under snow. They are specially trained to carry first aid to the trapped person and to stay with them, if necessary, until help arrives. Shepherds have also used dogs for centuries to round up sheep.

Search dogs are considered to be the most highly trained canines in the world

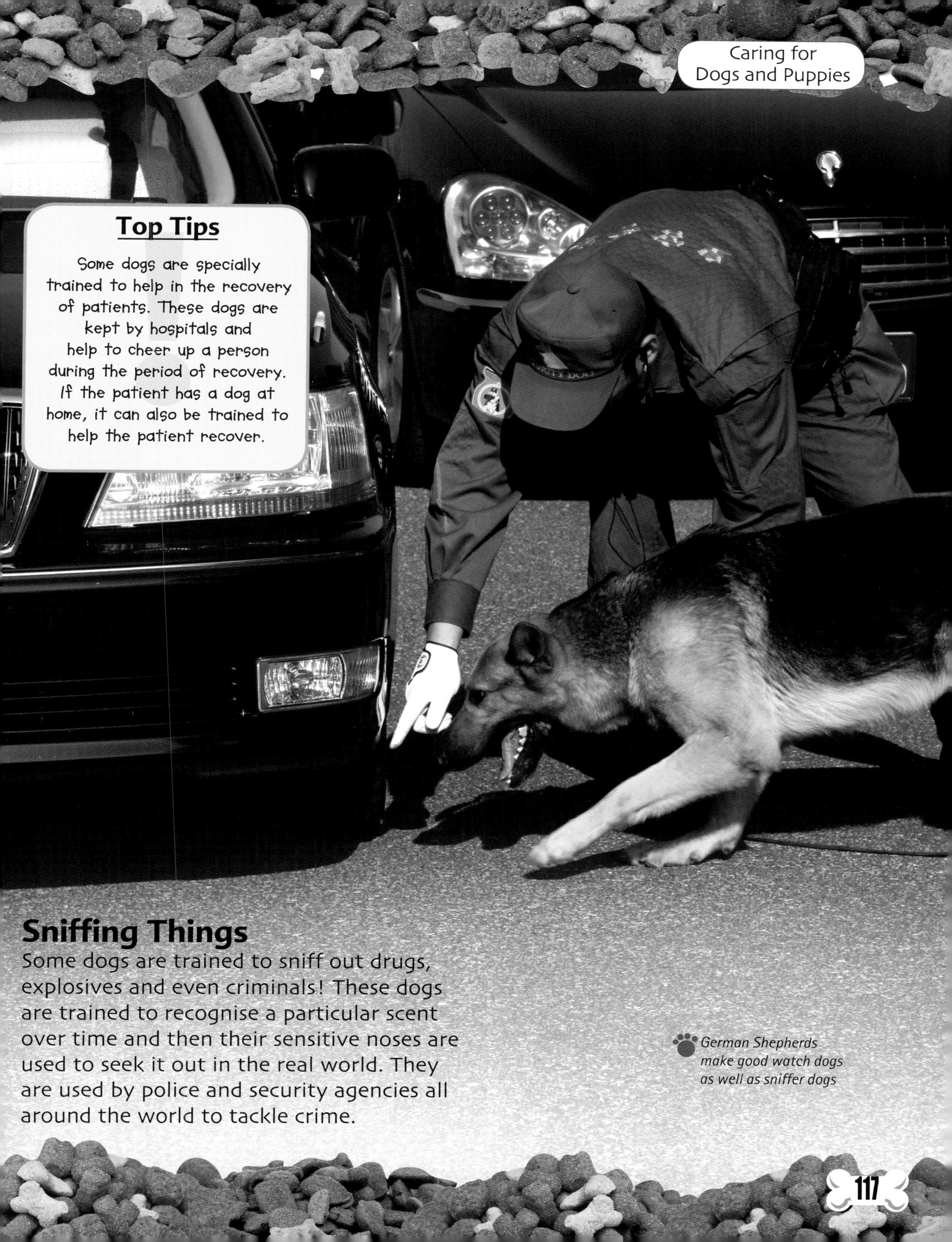

Top Tips

Some dogs are specially trained to help in the recovery of patients. These dogs are kept by hospitals and help to cheer up a person during the period of recovery. If the patient has a dog at home, it can also be trained to help the patient recover.

Sniffing Things

Some dogs are trained to sniff out drugs, explosives and even criminals! These dogs are trained to recognise a particular scent over time and then their sensitive noses are used to seek it out in the real world. They are used by police and security agencies all around the world to tackle crime.

German Shepherds make good watch dogs as well as sniffer dogs

Household Dangers

There are many things in your house that can cause harm to your dog or puppy. You have to take precautions and guard your pet against these dangers.

Poison

Poison for rats and cockroaches, as well as insecticides, should be kept out of reach of pets. If they mistake it for food and eat it, they can be very ill, or can even die. It is also advisable to keep medicines out of their reach. Also remember to not give any chocolate to your pet. In large quantities, chocolates can poison it!

Always label jars in the house as a safety measure

In The Garden

Plants in your garden must be selected carefully. They should not contain any substance that may cause your dog or puppy harm. You must make sure that there is no chemical fertiliser or pesticide in the garden that is within reach of your pet. If your pet consumes any of it then take it to the vet immediately.

Fertilisers or pesticides are potentially very dangerous to your dog or puppy

Choking Hazard

All dogs love bones, but you have to make sure your pet does not get any cooked or old bones, as they can crack into small splinters and choke the dog or puppy. For the same reason, never give your pet the bone of a chicken or any other bird. When you buy chewy toys for your pet, make sure these toys do not have removable small parts. These parts can choke a dog or puppy if swallowed.

Common Questions

Is antifreeze dangerous to pets?

Antifreeze contains a sweet chemical called ethylene glycol. This can attract animals. But antifreeze is very poisonous so keep it out of reach.

Treat your dog or puppy like a small child and always give it things that can be chewed easily without causing any harm

Vet and Vaccination

It is important to have a fixed vet who is familiar with your dog or puppy. You should take your pet for regular medical check-ups and vaccinations.

Selecting a Vet

Ask any friends or relatives who have a dog or puppy to recommend a good vet. Then, before you bring your pet home, visit the vet and satisfy yourself that they and their team are suitable to treat your dog or puppy. Your vetinerary surgery should be open to you looking round and asking any questions you have, but be careful not to interupt their work. Once you have bought your dog or puppy, book an initial consultation with your vet as soon as possible.

The Adviser

Even when your pet is perfectly healthy, the vet is your adviser about a number of things, like the kind of food you should give, the kind of housing needed, the training of your pet and where to leave your pet if you are going on a holiday. So stay in touch with your vet.

Always consult an adult before you finalise a vet for your dog or puppy

Vaccines

It is important to get your dog or puppy vaccinated as soon as you bring it home. A proper vaccination programme protects your pet and everyone else at home. The programme will vary from breed to breed and your vet will explain exactly what your dog or puppy needs. The dog or puppy may initially react to a vaccine. It may sleep for many hours at a stretch or lose its appetite for some time. Ask your vet about possible reactions, so that you are not scared without reason.

Follow your vet's vaccination schedule closely. This will help your pet become familiar with the vet and will keep them healthy

Top Tips

Some dogs or puppies may react to vaccines more strongly than others. Do alert your vet if this happens to your pet, but this is no reason to stop the vaccination programme.

GLOSSARY

Abscess: A swelling with pus

Administer: To give or apply

Aggressive: Angry and violent

Agility: Physical and mental speed

Anesthesia: A drug given to make a body part numb

Antiseptic: Substance applied to reduce chance of infection

Appetite: Desire to eat

Assess: To evaluate

Bovine: Family of cows

Breed: Particular species

Castrated: Removal of male reproductive organs of animals

Choking: Causing suffocation

Clipping: Trimming the body hair of horses and ponies

Communicate: To convey one's feeling

Constitution: Physical build

Contagion: Communication of disease from one person to another

Dehydration: Loss of water

Dismount: To get off a horse or pony

Docile: Timid

Domesticate: To bring animals under human control

Draught animals: Animals used for pulling heavy loads

Equine: Relating to the horse family

Endurance: Ability to bear hardship

Exhaustion: Tiredness

Fertilizer: A chemical added to soil to increase its fertility

Fleas: Small insects that suck blood from animals

Foal: Young horse

Founder: A disease causing lameness

Frostbite: Injury from exposure to freezing temperatures

Grooming: Cleaning

Harness: To hold something in place with straps

Hygienic: Free from germs and diseases

Hyperactive: Excessively active

GLOSSARY

Incubate: Keeping eggs warm to allow them to hatch better

Infestation: Germs and disease causing organisms on the body or in a place

Irritable: Easily annoyed

Kennel: House for a dog

Legumes: Plants belonging to the pea family

Longevity: Long life

Lunging: The process where you stand while you have your horse lope or trot, or even walk, around you in a circle

Malnourished: In bad health due to lack of food

Mishap: Accident

Morose: Sad

Muck out: Clearing out the dung from the stable

Paddock: A small field where horses are kept

Pasture: Land covered mainly with grass suitable for grazing

Precautions: Safety measures

Predatory: Living by feeding on other animals

Prey: Animals that are hunted

Prospect: Possibility of any future event

Purr: Soft call of the cat

Replenish: To restore back to original state

Saline: Sterile saltwater mixture

Serpentine: Winding and twisting

Stamina: Energy

Symptoms: Signs

Temperament: Character

Threatened: Feeling unsafe

Thrifty: Avoiding waste

Ticks: Blood sucking insects that are a little larger than fleas

Unruly: Badly behaved

Vaccines: Injections to prevent diseases

Vet: A doctor who treats animals

Weaning: Moving a baby from mother's milk to solid food

Yield: Given amount

INDEX

INDEX